D0454047

Being Fluent

with INFORMATION TECHNOLOGY

Committee on Information Technology Literacy

Computer Science and Telecommunications Board
Commission on Physical Sciences, Mathematics, and Applications
National Research Council

NATIONAL ACADEMY PRESS
Washington, D.C.

T

Support for this project was provided by the National Science Foundation under Contract Number CDA-9616681. Any opinions, findings, conclusions, or recommendations expressed in this material are those of the authors and do not necessarily reflect the views of the sponsor.

Library of Congress Catalog Card Number 99-63379
International Standard Book Number 0-309-06399-X

Additional copies of this report are available from:

National Academy Press, 2101 Constitution Avenue, NW, Box 285, Washington, DC 20055
800/624-6242, 202/334-3313 (in the Washington metropolitan area), http://www.nap.edu

First Printing, June 1999
Second Printing, September 1999

v

Preface

In response to a request from the National Science Foundation, the Computer Science and Telecommunications Board (CSTB) of the National Research Council initiated a study in August 1997 to address the subject of information technology literacy. The rationale for such a study was that the increasing importance and ubiquity of information technology in daily life make it essential to articulate what everyone needs to know and understand about information technology. Such an articulation would be an essential first step toward empowering all citizens to participate in the information age.

Information technology as a topic for literacy has multiple constituencies. For example, the library science community has developed a conceptual underpinning for skills that are important for finding, evaluating, and using information, all of which are important aspects of any definition of information technology literacy. Because they spend their professional lives as creators of information technology, computer scientists have their own perspectives, as do practitioners in disciplines that have traditionally relied on computational tools, such as science and engineering. Disciplines in the arts and humanities are just beginning to tap the potential of information technology and will become (indeed, some would argue are now) important stakeholders. More generally, the broad category "knowledge worker" encompasses many professions in the workplace, and virtually all knowledge workers make use in greater and lesser degrees (increasingly greater) of information technology. Traditionally "blue-collar" workers such as auto mechanics and heating/air-conditioning technicians must also cope with a proliferation of embedded computing devices. And as government begins to provide more services to the public using information technology, the citizenry itself becomes an interested constituent.

THE COMMITTEE'S APPROACH

In addressing its charge, the committee chose a broad definition of information technology. Information technology was defined to include the more traditional components of information technology (such as general-purpose computational devices, associated peripherals, operating environments, applications software, and information), as well as embedded computing devices, communications, and the science underlying the technology.

As for the knowledge and understanding component of its charge, the committee decided to use the term "fluency." Professor Yasmin Kafai, who briefed the committee, noted that fluency connotes the ability to reformulate knowledge, to express oneself creatively and appropriately, and to produce and generate information (rather than simply to comprehend it). This report uses the term "fluency with information technology," or FITness, and it characterizes as fluent with information technology (FIT) those who use, understand, and know about information technology in the ways described in Chapter 2. Chapter 1 contrasts fluency with the more common term "literacy."

All of the committee believed in the social desirability of the broadest possible dissemination of a set of fundamental concepts, skills, and capabilities. Good arguments were made to and by the committee for defining "everyone" in terms of all junior high school graduates, all high school graduates, all non-college-bound individuals, all college-bound individuals, and all adult citizens (as lifelong learners). But in the end, rather than argue that FITness was required of everyone in some demographic category of the population, the committee instead chose to make its case for the education of individuals who want to be able to use information technology effectively. Furthermore, issues of committee expertise and budget imposed some practical constraints on the committee's work, and the committee decided that it was best qualified to focus, as a first step toward fuller implementation, on the group of learners with which it was most familiar—the four-year college or university graduate. This first step toward implementation is discussed in Chapter 4.

The intent of this report is to lay an intellectual framework for fluency with information technology that is useful for others in developing discipline-specific and/or grade-appropriate efforts to promote FITness. However, this report is not a FITness textbook, a curriculum for FITness, or even a description of standards for FITness.

METHODOLOGY

The committee sought input in three ways: through briefings on the topic from individuals who have worked in the field (Appendix C), from electronic input in response to a set of questions about FITness that the committee broadcast widely over the Internet, and from perspectives provided at an invitation-only workshop in Irvine, California, held to explore the subject, for which participants were sought from a broad range of backgrounds and interests (Appendix D). The committee, itself composed of individuals representing varied backgrounds and expertise (Appendix E), used this broad range of input in an integrative manner to inform its own deliberations on the appropriate scope and nature of FITness.

ACKNOWLEDGMENTS

The committee appreciates the sponsorship of the Cross-Disciplinary Activities of the Directorate for Computer and Information Science and Engineering of the National Science Foundation for this project, and especially the support of John Cherniavsky.

The committee benefited from input from a broad range of sources. A list of workshop participants is contained in Appendix D; a list of briefers is provided in Appendix C. Douglas Brown of Bellevue Community College and Mary Lindquist of Columbus State University provided useful comments on Chapter 2. Comments of reviewers (listed immediately following this preface) helped the committee to tighten its presentation and to determine the appropriate emphasis on the various topics contained in the report.

Acknowledgment of Reviewers

This report was reviewed by individuals chosen for their diverse perspectives and technical expertise, in accordance with procedures approved by the National Research Council's (NRC's) Report Review Committee. The purpose of this independent review is to provide candid and critical comments that will assist the authors and the NRC in making the published report as sound as possible and to ensure that the report meets institutional standards for objectivity, evidence, and responsiveness to the study charge. The contents of the review comments and draft manuscript remain confidential to protect the integrity of the deliberative process. We wish to thank the following individuals for their participation in the review of this report:

George Bugliarello, Polytechnic University,
Robert Patterson Cook, University of Mississippi,
Ronald Danielson, Santa Clara University,
Scot Drysdale, Dartmouth College,
John Hennessy, Stanford University,
Leah Jamison, Purdue University,
Joan Lippincott, Coalition for Networked Information,
Arthur Melmed, George Mason University,
Susan L. Perry, Mount Holyoke College,
Jane Prey, University of Virginia,
Harold Salzman, University of Massachusetts – Lowell, and
Kendall N. Starkweather, International Technology Education
    Association.

Although the individuals listed above provided many constructive comments and suggestions, responsibility for the final content of this report rests solely with the study committee and the NRC.

Contents

Executive Summary

Information technology is playing an increasingly important role in the work and personal lives of citizens. Computers, communications, digital information, software—the constituents of the information age—are everywhere.

Between those who search aggressively for opportunities to learn more about information technology and those who choose not to learn anything at all about information technology, there are many who recognize the potential value of information technology for their everyday lives and who realize that a better understanding of information technology will be helpful to them. This realization is based on several factors:

- Information technology has entered our lives over a relatively brief period of time with little warning and essentially no formal educational preparation for most people.
- Many who currently use information technology have only a limited understanding of the tools they use and a (probably correct) belief that they are underutilizing them.
- Many citizens do not feel confident or in control when confronted by information technology, and they would like to be more certain of themselves.
- There have been impressive claims for the potential benefits of information technology, and many would like to realize those benefits.
- There is concern on the part of some citizens that changes implied by information technology embody potential risks to social values, freedoms or economic interests, etc., obligating them to become informed.

And, naturally, there is simple curiosity about how this powerful and pervasive technology works.

These various motivations to learn more about information technology raise the general question, What should everyone know about information technology in order to use it more effectively now and in the future? Addressing that question is the subject of this report.

The answer to this question is complicated by the fact that information technology is changing rapidly. The electronic computer is just over 50 years old, "PC," as in personal computer, is less than 20 years old, and the World Wide Web has been known to the public for less than 5 years. In the presence of rapid change, it is impossible to give a fixed, once-and-for-all course that will remain current and effective.

Generally, "computer literacy" has acquired a "skills" connotation, implying competency with a few of today's computer applications, such as word processing and e-mail. Literacy is too modest a goal in the presence of rapid change, because it lacks the necessary "staying power." As the technology changes by leaps and bounds, existing skills become antiquated and there is no migration path to new skills. A better solution is for the individual to plan to adapt to changes in the technology. This involves learning sufficient foundational material to enable one to acquire new skills independently after one's formal education is complete.

This requirement of a deeper understanding than is implied by the rudimentary term "computer literacy" motivated the committee to adopt "fluency" as a term connoting a higher level of competency. People fluent with information technology (FIT persons) are able to express themselves creatively, to reformulate knowledge, and to synthesize new information. Fluency with information technology (i.e., what this report calls FITness) entails a process of lifelong learning in which individuals continually apply what they know to adapt to change and acquire more knowledge to be more effective at applying information technology to their work and personal lives.

Fluency with information technology requires three kinds of knowledge: contemporary skills, foundational concepts, and intellectual capabilities. These three kinds of knowledge prepare a person in different ways for FITness.

- Contemporary skills, the ability to use today's computer applications, enable people to apply information technology immediately. In the present labor market, skills are an essential component of job readiness. Most importantly, skills provide a store of practical experience on which to build new competence.
- Foundational concepts, the basic principles and ideas of comput-

ers, networks, and information, underpin the technology. Concepts explain the how and why of information technology, and they give insight into its opportunities and limitations. Concepts are the raw material for understanding new information technology as it evolves.

• Intellectual capabilities, the ability to apply information technology in complex and sustained situations, encapsulate higher-level thinking in the context of information technology. Capabilities empower people to manipulate the medium to their advantage and to handle unintended and unexpected problems when they arise. The intellectual capabilities foster more abstract thinking about information and its manipulation.

For specificity, the report enumerates the ten highest-priority items for each of the three types of knowledge. (Box ES.1 lists these ten items for each type of knowledge.) The skills, linked closely to today's computer usage, will change over time, but the concepts and capabilities are timeless.

Concepts, capabilities, and skills the three different types of knowledge of FITness—occupy separate dimensions, implying that a particular activity involving information technology will involve elements of each type of knowledge. Learning the skills and concepts and developing the intellectual capabilities can be undertaken without reference to each other, but such an effort will not promote FITness to any significant degree. The three elements of FITness are co-equal, each reinforcing the others, and all are essential to FITness.

FITness is personal in the sense that individuals fluent with information technology evaluate, distinguish, learn, and use new information technology as appropriate to their own personal and professional activities. What is appropriate for an individual depends on the particular applications, activities, and opportunities for being FIT that are associated with the individual's area of interest or specialization.

FITness is also graduated and dynamic. It is graduated in the sense that FITness is characterized by different levels of sophistication (rather than a single fluent/not fluent judgment). And, it is dynamic in that FITness entails lifelong learning as information technology evolves.

In short, FITness should not be regarded as an end state that is independent of domain, but rather as something that develops over a lifetime in particular domains of interest and that has a different character and tone depending on which domains are involved. Accordingly, the pedagogic goal is to provide students with a sufficiently complete foundation of the three types of knowledge that they can "learn the rest of it" on their own as the need arises throughout life.

Because FITness is fundamentally integrative, calling upon an indi-

Box ES.1
The Components of Fluency with Information Technology

NOTE: Readers are urged to read Chapter 2 for more elaboration of these items.

Intellectual Capabilities

1. Engage in sustained reasoning.
2. Manage complexity.
3. Test a solution.
4. Manage problems in faulty solutions.
5. Organize and navigate information structures and evaluate information.
6. Collaborate.
7. Communicate to other audiences.
8. Expect the unexpected.
9. Anticipate changing technologies.
10. Think about information technology abstractly.

Information Technology Concepts

1. Computers
2. Information systems
3. Networks
4. Digital representation of information
5. Information organization
6. Modeling and abstraction
7. Algorithmic thinking and programming
8. Universality
9. Limitations of information technology
10. Societal impact of information and information technology

Information Technology Skills

1. Setting up a personal computer
2. Using basic operating system features
3. Using a word processor to create a text document
4. Using a graphics and/or artwork package to create illustrations, slides, or other image-based expressions of ideas
5. Connecting a computer to a network
6. Using the Internet to find information and resources
7. Using a computer to communicate with others
8. Using a spreadsheet to model simple processes or financial tables
9. Using a database system to set up and access useful information
10. Using instructional materials to learn how to use new applications or features

vidual to coordinate information and skills with respect to multiple dimensions of a problem and to make overall judgments and decisions taking all such information into account, a project-based approach to developing FITness is most appropriate. Projects of appropriate scale and scope inherently involve multiple iterations, each of which provides an opportunity for an instructional checkpoint or intervention. The domain of a project can be tailored to an individual's interest (e.g., in the department of a student's major), thereby providing motivation for a person to expend the (non-trivial) effort to master the concepts and skills of FITness. In addition, a project of appropriate scope will be sufficiently complex that intellectual integration is necessary to complete it. Note also that much of the infrastructure of existing skills-based computer or information technology literacy efforts (e.g., hardware, software, network connections, support staff) will be important elements of efforts to promote FITness.

Although the essentials of FITness are for the most part not dependent on sophisticated mathematics, and should therefore generally be accessible in some form to every citizen, any program or effort to make individuals more FIT must be customized to the target population. Because the committee was composed of college and university faculty, the committee chose to focus its implementational concerns on the four-year college or university graduate as one important starting point for the development of FITness across the citizenry. Further, the committee believes that successful implementation of FITness instruction will require serious rethinking of the college and university curriculum. It will not be sufficient for individual instructors to revisit their course content or approach. Rather, entire departments must examine the question of the extent to which their students will graduate FIT. Universities need to concern themselves with the FITness of students who cross discipline boundaries and with the extent to which each discipline is meeting the goals of universal FITness.

In summary, FIT individuals, those who know a starter set of information technology skills, who understand the basic concepts on which information technology is founded, and who have engaged in the higher-level thinking embodied in the intellectual capabilities, should use information technology confidently, should come to work ready to learn new business systems quickly and use them effectively, should be able to apply information technology to personally relevant problems, and should be able to adapt to the inevitable change as information technology evolves over their lifetime. To be FIT is to possess knowledge essential to using information technology now and in the future.

1

Why Know About
Information Technology?

This report focuses on what an individual must know and understand about information technology in order to use it effectively and productively for his or her own purposes. There are at least four broad categories of rationale motivating an understanding of information technology: personal, workforce, educational, and societal.

1.1 PERSONAL RATIONALES

America is increasingly an information society. Computers and communications not only perform routine tasks like controlling microwave ovens and connecting cellular phones, but with the Internet they give the computer-capable among us access to much of the world's digital information and the means to process it. From finding a subway map of Prague for vacation planning to locating the best buys for books, mortgages, and cowboy boots, many Americans find that the use of information technology is a valuable enhancement to their way of life. Information technology helps people to keep in contact with family and friends via e-mail, manage their finances with spreadsheets and online banking, track investments through an online broker, pursue hobbies like genealogy or gardening with specialized software packages, help their children with homework and school projects using word processing and graphing tools, find medical information, become informed about political candidates and communicate with their political representatives, and track environmental issues or monitor public policy issues over the World Wide Web.

1.2   A WORKFORCE RATIONALE

In today's workplace, information technology is increasingly common. If the nation is to obtain the maximum benefit from its investments in information technology, a labor pool capable of using it appropriately is necessary. It is obvious that individuals who work with information and knowledge (so-called "knowledge workers") need to understand the ubiquitous office information technologies, but it is also true that few job classifications require no knowledge of information technology at all. For example, the clerk in a retail establishment at one time had only to know how to use a cash register. Today, the same clerk can come into contact with inventory systems, order tracking, and credit card and other business systems, which are becoming more sophisticated and integrated. In the manufacturing industry, many traditionally "blue-collar" workers must cope with a variety of manufacturing systems for tracking materials, parts inventory and production, process control, and online manuals and procedures.

Though a company must train its employees in the use of its business systems, it is naïve to consider such training as a one time activity. The systems are upgraded frequently and become more complex. Opportunities to apply information technology to business problems and opportunities to integrate existing information technology solutions continue, implying a continual training mission. Obviously, this training task is greatly simplified if the labor pool is already well educated in information technology, since employees come up to speed faster and require less training overall. Further, they will probably utilize existing systems more fully and adapt to upgrades better. Employee productivity is directly affected by the employees' knowledge of information technology.

From the employee's point of view expertise in information technology is valuable. It not only leads to the simple satisfaction of performing one's job well and nimbly responding to problems; it can also improve job mobility. More facility with a company's information technology infrastructure can be a valuable job asset that may be considered in promotions. Finding a job at another company will entail learning new information systems, but understanding them more abstractly—knowing which features should be common and how they might differ—is also an asset in a labor market where employees no longer enjoy a "job for life."

1.3   AN EDUCATIONAL RATIONALE

Information technology is an enabler for many new types of educational opportunities. One type is based on the access of students to an array of educational resources that were not previously accessible to them.

Consider, for example, the Kids as Global Scientists program, operated by the University of Colorado in conjunction with the University of Michigan's Weather Underground and the Weather Channel. The goal of this program is to help students use the Internet to learn about weather and environmental science issues as they also get to know other students from different regions of the United States and the world. The program and associated curriculum offer student-directed discussions and predictions about the paths and history of this year's tropical storms that can be compared with those of the experts and with the actual event as it occurs; hands-on activities, real-time data collection, and instructions on how to view and interpret a variety of satellite images; guided access to interactive displays of current hurricane data and trajectories; links to newspaper stories and other current reports; student-collected data that is posted to the Internet to share with other classrooms around the world; content expertise from hurricane specialists via online questioning and conferencing; online discussion groups for teachers, students, and experts, providing support on technical, content, and pedagogical issues; and a vehicle for posting information and graphics about a student's school in an online newspaper.[1]

A second type of educational opportunity is described by MIT computer scientist Seymour Papert. In "Mindstorms," Papert asserts that a deep understanding of programming, in particular the notions of successive decomposition as a mode of analysis and debugging of trial solutions, results in significant educational benefits in many domains of discourse, including those unrelated to computers and information technology per se.[2] He further argues that computers can be the means for educators "to support the development of new ways of thinking and learning" (p. xiv). He believes that computers can be a conduit of powerful ideas and "the seeds of cultural change, . . . help[ing] people form new relationships with knowledge that cuts across the traditional lines separating humanities from sciences and knowledge of the self . . ." (p. 4). By transforming abstractions into concrete representations via programming, students "build their own intellectual structures with materials drawn from surrounding culture" (pp. 31-32).

Finally, a third type of opportunity is the medium that information technology provides for students to develop and exercise their critical thinking abilities. Information conveyed through advanced information

---

[1]For more information, see <http://www.onesky.umich.edu/kgs/htdocs/home1.html>.
[2]Seymour A. Papert. 1999. *Mindstorms: Children, Computers, and Powerful Ideas*, Second Edition, Basic Books, New York.

technology such as computers and the World Wide Web can appear more convincing than the same information conveyed through a conversation with a stranger or the newspaper, despite the fact that it may have equivalent accuracy and validity. Students must evaluate all information critically. Their ability to present information using information technology can aid in developing an ability to separate form from content in all information, and in assessing its accuracy and validity. The result is a more critical evaluation of all information. Such critical ability helps individuals to evaluate information technology-mediated claims for alternative medicines, advertisements for energy-efficient homes, and homework advice from peers.

1.4 A SOCIETAL RATIONALE

The practice of democracy is based on an informed citizenry. In today's increasingly technological society, many public policy debates are connected to information technology. For example:

• A person with a basic understanding of database technology can better appreciate the risks to privacy entailed in data-mining based on his or her credit-card transactions.

• A jury that understands the basics of computer animation and image manipulation may have a better understanding of what counts as "photographic truth" in the reconstruction of a crime or an accident.

• Understanding choices about representation of information can be key to understanding how copyright laws may apply to information in electronic media.

• A person who understands the structure and operation of the World Wide Web is in a better position to evaluate and appreciate policy issues related to the First Amendment, free expression, and the availability of pornography on the Internet.

While some of these issues were argued and debated before the advent of modern information technology, the pervasiveness of information technology has brought many of them into the public consciousness in a more poignant and vivid manner. Some basic understanding of information technology thus is needed to make informed judgments about these public policy issues, many of which have a direct impact on citizens whether or not they use information technology in their daily lives.

As information technology becomes more and more ubiquitous, citizens need to know how to evaluate the social impact of information technology and when to complain about information technology solutions embedded in their lives. The "Year 2000" problem reminds citizens, technology experts, government policy makers, and industry leaders that seemingly transparent technological solutions can have substantial weaknesses. Citizens who live in a world where information technology grows, changes, advances, and fails require some level of understanding of information technology if they are to make informed choices.

Finally, entirely apart from public policy concerns per se, the growing use of information technology throughout the world may have profound social effects (Box 1.1).

1.5   UNDERSTANDING, KNOWING, AND USING INFORMATION TECHNOLOGY

This report asserts that individuals must understand information technology in order to use it effectively. This assertion may seem to be curious advice considering that the foregoing rationales argue substantial benefits already exist from the use of information technology even for individuals who lack an enhanced understanding of the topic. Further, industry is eager to make information technologies as easy to use as possible. Why should there be anything more to learn?

Though both observations have some truth, they overlook several critical points about current and future uses of information technology.

•   Almost by definition, new technologies have not yet been deeply explored, and applications or products or services based on new technologies are often fragile, quirky, unintuitive, and flawed. (The same qualities may also beset applications or products or services based on relatively old technologies!) An understanding of the underlying technologies helps the user to cope with the difficulties inevitably encountered in use.

•   The information technology needs of an individual may not be met by an off-the-shelf application, implying that it may not be possible to fulfill needs simply by punching a single button (as individuals might in using a specialized information "appliance"). Thus, having some understanding of information technology will help individuals make more effective use of whatever technology is available to them.

•   The ability to use a tool in a rudimentary manner for a limited set of purposes is not the same as the ability to use the tool safely, effectively, and flexibly. The former may be sufficient for many individuals, but the more an individual possesses the latter ability, the more useful the tool is to that individual.

•   New information technologies and applications of that technology emerge rapidly. In some cases, the power and capabilities of new developments will be well matched to the needs of a particular individual. An individual who has a robust understanding of information technology will be able to exploit these developments and to comprehend the capabilities and implications of new technologies more quickly.

• Many people approach computers tentatively and with little confidence, even if they have been using computers for years. This seeming paradox probably derives from the fact that they have little true understanding of the technology. The training for the applications they know has concentrated on using the tools, and has ignored more general description of principles and concepts. When something goes wrong, or a new application is available, people with such backgrounds are at a loss to know what to do and often experience frustration. They must get help, further adding to their feeling of not being in control, and the help they receive usually treats the immediate problem without imparting more basic knowledge, thus perpetuating the problem.

Granting that some knowledge of information technology is necessary for its use, many efforts have focused on what has come to be known as "computer literacy." This term has a long history, and in common parlance it means the ability to use a few computer applications. For example, computer literacy often refers to the ability to use a spreadsheet and a word processor and to search the World Wide Web for information. In an era in which the most useful applications change rapidly, the "skills" approach lacks "staying power." New tools or new versions of tools emerge frequently, requiring new skills. For example, searching the World Wide Web would not have been a skill included in a literacy course five years ago. Skills with specific applications are thus necessary but not sufficient for individuals to prosper in the information age.

The following analogy illustrates one difference between "computer literacy" and the robust understanding of information technology described in Chapter 2. Consider a person who has visited a certain city several times and who has learned a single route from the airport to some final destination. This visitor's understanding of the local geography is limited and fragile, whereas residents have a fuller understanding of arterial streets and landmarks. When a traffic jam occurs, the visitor doubtless chooses to wait it out, while the resident is more able to find an alternate route. Though the resident may not necessarily be familiar with the local streets of the exit, knowing the landmarks and general organization of the arterials will allow a rapid recovery. In the same way, a computer-literate individual knowing only basic information technology skills—word processing, e-mail, simple Web browsing—may appear not to need a deep or robust understanding of information technology, but when faced with an unexpected event or a problem, may well be less able to adapt or to find a work-around.

Box 1.1
Possible Social Effects of Information Technology

Information technology has brought or is bringing more abstract or intangible changes than those enumerated in the text.

•   *Freedom.* Information technology is an enabler for the opportunity for individuals to express themselves freely, unfettered by intermediaries. For a modest investment in a computer and the nominal cost of a connection to an Internet service provider, anyone can post anything on a personal home page or say anything in a chat room, and the potential audience for such postings is quite large. Such convenient, inexpensive, and sustained opportunities for free speech are unprecedented, as are the dark sides of easy expression (e.g., the ease of disseminating misinformation or disinformation, hate speech, child pornography, and so on).

•   *World connectivity.* Information technology is cheap, fast, "point to point," and asynchronous, giving e-mail a convenience and immediacy that postal and telephonic communications have never had, and a personalization that broadcast media cannot provide. With the World Wide Web, access to local information is possible at unprecedented speeds—one can read the Sydney Morning Herald in Sydney, Nova Scotia, at the same moment that Australians are reading it. The ease with which information technology allows citizens of the world to keep in touch with people and events elsewhere unifies the world profoundly. And this effect will increase as information technology becomes adopted more completely around the world.

•   *Loss of remoteness.* A corollary to the world-connecting property of information technology is that information resources are now much more accessible to individuals worldwide. Although the entire holdings of the New York Public Library will not soon be completely online, the informa-

1.6   FLUENCY WITH INFORMATION TECHNOLOGY

This report addresses the question, What must an individual know and understand about information technology in order to use it effectively and productively for his or her own purposes? Because the technology is changing continually (and rapidly), the answer to this question cannot be static. The rapid pace of change in information technology—electronic computers are barely 50 years old, the term "PC" is less than 20 years old, and the World Wide Web has been known to the public for less than 5— implies that neither a fixed repertoire of skills nor a static curriculum taught "once and for all" can possibly suffice.

tion access advantages of those living in geographically remote areas with access to the World Wide Web compare favorably to those living in the Big Apple. The information needed by many people, though perhaps not scholars, is largely available electronically. Telecommuting is another manifestation of information technology's location independence.

• *Alienation.* There is recent, preliminary evidence that even a modest amount of time (one or a few hours per day) spent on the Internet can lead some users to feelings of depression and alienation.[1] An apparent source of some alienation is that "friendships" formed via chat rooms can be more superficial than those formed through face-to-face interaction. In addition, the time spent in front of a screen reduces normal interpersonal contact. This topic requires further study, and if the findings of the Carnegie Mellon University study are confirmed, would suggest the need for attention to the mental health consequences of changes associated with the use of information technology.

• *Predominance of English.* Information technology is largely an English-oriented medium, because its development has followed the English-centric tradition of post-World War II science, and, perhaps more importantly, because the United States has played a dominant role in the deployment of information technology. While information in almost every written language can be found on the World Wide Web, a surfer must have at least a passable understanding of English to reap the greatest advantage of information technology globally. The implications for other natural languages are unclear, but it is likely that many world residents will want to be bilingual in the near future.

---

[1] Robert Kraut et al. 1998. "Internet Paradox: A Social Technology That Reduces Social Involvement and Psychological Well-Being?", *American Psychologist*, 53(9):1017-1031.

And, because the technology is powerful, the answer to the question cannot be superficial. If effectively using information technology were as simple as driving a car or using an automatic teller machine, it would be easy to teach what one would need to know about information technology in order to use it. But computers and communication are more versatile and in a deep sense more powerful technologies, making the educational task more challenging. (Chapter 2 grounds this assertion in more precise terms, and explicitly addresses the oft-mentioned analogy between driving and computing.)

While some applications of information technology require relatively little knowledge to use, other quite useful applications are accessible only to those who have some understanding of the underlying technology. Those who have this understanding, perhaps because they are technically trained, acquired it in connection with their work, or are simply curious, motivated, and persistent enough to have figured it out on their own, have greater facility operating in the digital world and thus greater access to the benefits it offers.

While no term is perfect, the notion of *fluency* captures best for the committee connotations of the ability to reformulate knowledge, to express oneself creatively and appropriately, and to produce and generate information (rather than simply to comprehend it). For this reason, the committee chose "fluency with information technology," or FITness, as a label for the robust understanding of what is needed to use information technology effectively across a broad range of applications.

FITness involves three distinct but interrelated dimensions—intellectual capabilities, conceptual knowledge, and an appropriate skill set. An individual who develops these capabilities, knowledge, and skills becomes more fluent with information technology (FIT). Functionally, a more FIT individual is better able to use today's information technology effectively in personal and professional life, to adapt information technology to be personally relevant, and to acquire future knowledge as information technology changes than a person who is less FIT. An adequate level of FITness provides an individual with the foundational knowledge and understanding that enable him or her to advance along a continuum, becoming more and more adept at applying information technology for a range of purposes and having a deeper understanding of the technological opportunities for doing so.

In Chapter 2, each of these dimensions of FITness is defined and explained more carefully. Chapter 2 outlines the intellectual core of FITness. Chapter 3 discusses several collateral issues associated with the FITness framework. Chapter 4 addresses "implementational efforts," which are necessarily tied to specific grade levels. In the case of this report, they are tied to college undergraduates.

2

The Intellectual Framework of Fluency with Information Technology

2.1 WHAT IS FLUENCY WITH INFORMATION TECHNOLOGY?

Fluency with information technology (abbreviated as FITness) goes beyond traditional notions of computer literacy. As noted in Chapter 1, literacy about information technology might call for a minimal level of familiarity with technological tools like word processors, e-mail, and Web browsers. By contrast, FITness requires that persons understand information technology broadly enough to be able to apply it productively at work and in their everyday lives, to recognize when information technology would assist or impede the achievement of a goal, and to continually adapt to the changes in and advancement of information technology. FITness therefore requires a deeper, more essential understanding and mastery of information technology for information processing, communication, and problem solving than does computer literacy as traditionally defined. (Box 2.1 addresses the difference between literacy and FITness in more specific terms.) Note also that FITness as described in this chapter builds on many other fundamental competencies, such as textual literacy, logical reasoning, and knowledge of civics and society.

Information technology is a medium that permits the expression of a vast array of information, ideas, concepts, and messages, and FITness is about effectively exploiting that expressive power. FITness enables a person to accomplish a variety of different tasks using information technology and to develop different ways of accomplishing a given task.

FITness comes in degrees and gradations and is tied to different pur-

---

Box 2.1
I Use Computers All Day—Am I FIT?

Many Americans use information technology daily in their work, but such contact does not automatically bestow fluency with information technology. Although many jobs—medical records data entry, submitting credit card transactions, building spreadsheets in an accounting department, designing homes using architectural computer-aided design tools, and numerous others—require facility with the tools provided by specific information technology systems, this kind of expertise is often restricted largely to the skills dimension of FITness. Developing FITness as described in this report requires more than sustained contact with information technology, though such experience can nevertheless provide a good point of departure. Common fears about "breaking something" will have been overcome, certain common protocols will have been learned, and unusual situations will have been encountered.

There are highly FIT individuals across America and the world, of course. Through a combination of classes, experience, reading, curiosity, and probably persistence, these individuals not only have acquired skills that make information technology useful in their work and personal lives, but they also have learned a base of concepts and intellectual capabilities sufficient to acquire new knowledge about information technology independently, allowing them to expand their use and to adapt to change. Some are "techies," but many are simply individuals who by various means have gained enough basic knowledge to become independent, lifelong learners. As they learn more, they become more FIT, more adept at applying information technology to personally relevant tasks.

---

poses. FITness is thus not an "end state" that is independent of domain, but rather develops over a lifetime in particular domains of interest involving particular applications. Aspects of FITness can be developed by using spreadsheets for personal or professional budgeting, desktop publishing tools to create or edit documents or Web pages, search engines and database management tools for locating information on the Web or in large databases, and design tools to create visualizations in various scientific and engineering disciplines.

The wide variety of contexts in which FITness is relevant is matched by the rapid pace at which information technology evolves. Most professionals today require constant upgrading of technological skills as new tools become useful in their work; they learn new word processing programs, new computer-assisted design environments, or new techniques for searching the World Wide Web. Different applications of information technology emerge rather frequently, both in areas with long traditions of using information and information technology and in areas that are not usually seen as being technology-intensive. Perhaps the major challenge for individuals embarking on the goal of lifelong FITness involves deciding when to learn a new tool, when to change to a new technology, when to devote energy to increasing technological competency, and when to allocate time to other professional activities.

The above comments suggest that FITness is personal, graduated, and dynamic. FITness is personal in the sense that individuals evaluate, distinguish, learn, and use new information technology as appropriate to their own sustained personal and professional activities. What is appropriate for an individual depends on the particular applications, activities, and opportunities for FITness that are associated with the individual's area of interest or specialization, and what is reasonable for a FIT lawyer or a historian to know and be able to do may well differ from what is required for a FIT scientist or engineer. FITness is graduated in the sense that it is characterized by different levels of sophistication (rather than a single FIT/not-FIT judgment), and it is dynamic in that it requires lifelong learning as information technology evolves.

Put differently, FITness should not be assessed according to whether a person "has/does not have" all ten capabilities, and is not a single "pass/fail judgment." People with different needs and interests and goals will have lesser or greater stakes in the various components of FITness— they will obviously have greater stakes in those components that are most directly linked to their own individual needs. Nevertheless, the committee believes that all of the elements discussed below are necessary for individuals to exploit effectively the power of information technology across even a relatively small range of interests and needs.

2.2   THE ELEMENTS OF FITness

FITness involves three types of knowledge. These types, described briefly below, interact to reinforce each other, leading to deeper understanding of information technology and its uses.

- *Intellectual capabilities.* The intellectual capabilities of FITness refer to one's ability to apply information technology in complex and sustained situations and to understand the consequences of doing so. These capabilities transcend particular hardware or software applications. Indeed, the items listed as capabilities in Section 2.4 have general applicability to many domains other than information technology. But a great deal of research (and everyday experience as well) indicates that these capabilities do not easily transfer between problem domains,[1] and in general, few individuals are equally adept with these capabilities in all domains. For this reason, these capabilities can be regarded as "life skills" that are formulated in the context of information technology.

• *Fundamental concepts.* Concepts refer to the foundations on which information technology is built. This is the "book learning" part of fluency, although it is highly doubtful that a decent understanding of the concepts described in Section 2.5 can be achieved strictly through the use of textbooks. The concepts are fundamental to information and computing and are enduring in the sense that new concepts may become important in the future as qualitatively new information technologies emerge, but the presented list of fundamental concepts will be augmented with rather than replaced by new concepts.

• *Contemporary skills.* Skills refer to the ability to use particular (and contemporary) hardware or software resources to accomplish information processing tasks. Skills embody the intent of the phrase "knowing how to use a computer" as that phrase is colloquially understood. Skills include (but are not limited to) the use of several common software applications. The "skills" component of FITness necessarily changes over time because the information technology products and services available to citizens continually change. The enumeration given in Section 2.6 is appropriate for today, but the list would have been different five years ago and will surely be different five years from now.

Section 2.3 discusses the relationship of capabilities, concepts, and skills, as well as the role of knowledge in particular domains.

Intellectual capabilities and fundamental concepts of information technology are instantiated in or relevant to a wide variety of contexts. Intellectual capabilities and skills relate to very practical matters, getting at the heart of what it means to function in a complex technology-oriented world. And all have the characteristic that the acquisition of information technology skills, the understanding of information technology concepts, and the development of intellectual capabilities are lifelong activities. Over a lifetime, an individual will acquire more skills and develop additional proficiency with those skills, understand information technology

---

[1]See for example, National Research Council. 1999. *How People Learn: Brain, Mind, Experience, and School,* Chapter 3, "Learning and Transfer," National Academy Press, Washington, D.C.

concepts in a richer and more textured manner, and enhance his or her intellectual capabilities through engagement in multiple domains.

The discussion below proposes a "top ten" in each classification. (The ten are not listed in any order of priority.) Experts will doubtless recognize omissions and the list could easily be extended. But it is easy to generate longer lists, and at some point, the length of a list exceeds need, practicality, and even feasibility. The committee believes that it is important to identify the items of highest significance among possible alternatives, and the ten items in each category represent the committee's collective judgment of the most important. It is the committee's hope that all who draw from, build on, critique, or modify these lists will also impose a limit of ten on themselves.

2.3   A TRIPARTITE APPROACH TO FITness

Capabilities, concepts, and skills—the three different types of knowledge basic to FITness—occupy separate dimensions, implying that a particular activity involving information technology will involve elements of each type of knowledge. Learning information technology skills and concepts and developing the intellectual capabilities can be undertaken without reference to each other, but such an effort will not promote FITness to any significant degree. The three elements of FITness are co-equal, each reinforcing the others, and all are essential to FITness.[2]

• Study that emphasizes skills without fundamental concepts and intellectual capabilities meets some needs for utility in the short term. But although these skills enable one to perform basic tasks with a word processor (for example), they may not help much in countering the frustration felt when the computer freezes, the printer cannot be accessed, or the paragraphs mysteriously develop new fonts. Similar frustration is often experienced by an individual learning a new word-processor. The fundamental concepts underlying information technology are the basis for a mental model of how a specific application is (or is not) working, a model that enables reflective thought about what might be done to fix a problem or how a new application might work. The capabilities of FITness enable a person to deal with unexpected consequences and make appropriate decisions about learning new features or new software, and they are nec-

---

[2]The statement that "concepts, capabilities, and skills are co-equal" applies only to their epistemological importance to FITness. It does not argue that the appropriate pedagogies for each type of knowledge are, or should be, identical. This point is addressed at somewhat greater length in Section 4.3.

essary for one to engage in any kind of sustained effort using information technology.

• Study of information technology concepts in isolation from skills or capabilities is reminiscent of computer science education in the days before computers became abundant. The concepts represent abstract information about deep and interesting phenomena. They are worthy of study for their inherent interest, like studying sub-atomic particles and the structure of matter. But taught in the context of skills and capabilities, concepts also become the foundation on which one codifies one's experience, abstracts to new situations, and reasons about information technology. As information technology changes, concepts provide the basis for adapting to the change, inasmuch as the new systems adhere to the same principles the old systems did. Further, concepts provide the raw material needed to engage in capability-based action such as engaging in sustained reasoning and managing complexity.

• Study that emphasizes capabilities at the expense of concepts and skills will lack the essential connection to information technology. Although the intellectual capabilities are quite general, their development in the context of FITness requires a substantive connection to information technology that is provided by exposure to the concepts and skills. For example, to learn to "debug" a program or test an application, students need to understand the concepts implemented in the artifact. To implement their designs and work with others they need communication and search skills.

FITness integrates skills, concepts, and capabilities into an effective understanding of information technology, enabling citizens to use information technology to solve personally relevant problems and apply their knowledge of information technology to new situations. This integration is an essential element for individuals to learn over a lifetime. Thus, a pedagogical approach that balances the treatment of these three elements is essential—this is the subject of Chapter 4.

2.4   INTELLECTUAL CAPABILITIES FOR FITness

Within the framework of FITness as described above, the intellectual capabilities integrate knowledge specific to information technology with problem domains of personal interest to individuals. Many of the capabilities on this "top ten" list might be familiar in other disciplines—engineering design, library science, or general education—or even from an understanding of what is needed to live a productive life. Indeed, no assertion is made that these capabilities are unique or "belong" to information technology. However, the prominence and importance of information technology in society today take them out of the world of the designer or engineering specialist and put them squarely in the lives and workspaces of us all.

The essential elements of FITness include the ability to:

1. *Engage in sustained reasoning.*

Sustained reasoning starts with defining and clarifying a problem. Understanding exactly what problem is to be solved and knowing when it has been solved are often the most difficult aspects of problem solving. And, because information technology will in general operate in the way in which one directs it to operate, rather than the way in which one intends it to operate, precise specification of the problem to be solved with information technology is even more critical for solving other types of problems.

Once the problem has been defined, multiple attempts at formulating a solution are often required. An initial solution is often revised or improved by iteration, which often causes a refinement in the definition of the problem. Reasoning is used for planning, designing, executing, and evaluating a solution.

The "sustained" aspect of this capability is intended to convey an integrated effort that covers days or weeks rather than a one-time event. Thus, individuals might use desktop publishing programs, computer-assisted design tools, visualization and modeling environments, Web-search engines, or a variety of other technological resources to help implement a solution.

2. *Manage complexity.*

Problems often have a variety of solutions, each with its advantages and disadvantages, and trade-offs are often necessary in determining the most appropriate solution. One solution may require extensive design but result in a relatively straightforward implementation; another may require the opposite—a simple design but a costly implementation. Furthermore, any given approach to a solution will often result in components of a system interacting in complex, unexpected ways.

A sustained activity involving information technology will typically be complex, involving a number of tasks, such as problem clarification, solution formulation, solution design and implementation, and testing and evaluation of the outcome. The solution developed for the problem will often contain several components, including both hardware and software. A person needs to be able to plan a project, design a solution, integrate the components, respond to unexpected interactions, and diagnose what is needed from each task. Some of the steps of the project may involve some type of computer programming. Such programming could entail configuring system control panels, using and adapting existing software packages for one's needs, or writing code in some programming language.

Another source of complexity is the need to manage the resources that technology provides, especially when the resources available are inadequate. Thus, a user of information technology needs to be able to manage resources: Do processes require too much time? Too much disk space? Is the bandwidth available to download what is offered? And of course, are there ways to perform necessary tasks that will not exceed the limits imposed by resource availability and/or adequacy?

A third source of complexity is the fact that large information technology-based systems often have interdependencies. That is, small changes in one part of the system can have large effects on another part of the system that is "apparently" separate from that part. Such interdependencies can be reduced by enforcing a rigid separation between different system parts, but this practice is much easier to describe than to implement.

3. *Test a solution.*

Determining the scope, nature, and conditions under which a technological solution is intended to operate can be difficult. A solution to a problem must be tested in two ways—to determine that the design is correct or appropriate to the problem at hand (i.e., that the solution, when implemented correctly, will meet user needs) and to determine that the implementation of a given design is correct.

Testing entails determining whether a proposed solution meets design goals and works under diverse conditions, taking into account that most systems will be used in ways that were not intended, as well as in expected ways. Testing involves identifying the uses most likely to cause a failure, developing ways of testing for all normal modes of operation, determining typical misuses of the system, and designing the system so that it responds gracefully when misused. Furthermore, because some fixes to problems may introduce more problems, special care is necessary to fix (or manage) the initial flaws. Testing is also best seen as an activity concurrent with design, because the alternative is to implement a complete system before knowing whether the implementation is correct.

4. *Manage problems in faulty solutions.*

When systems crash and technological tools fail, users need the ability to "debug," that is, to detect, diagnose, and correct problems and faults (i.e., bugs). Debugging is a complex process that often goes beyond the technology and includes the personal and social aspects of the undertaking (e.g., when a system has multiple interacting components, each of which is the responsibility of a different individual). Debugging also involves other capabilites, such as sustained reasoning, managing complexity, and testing.

Debugging is necessary because the best-designed and best-integrated systems will still exhibit unanticipated behavior. Bugs are inevitably encountered in any ongoing effort using information technology, and thus users must anticipate the need to identify them, diagnose their sources (e.g., by recognizing patterns in observations or in fault reports, distinguishing root causes from derivative but proximate causes, and designing systematic diagnostic experiments), understand the implications of eliminating those sources, and take steps to modify the system appropriately. Alternatively, the appropriate response to a faulty system that is vital to some application may well be to structure the environment in which the system operates to limit the risk associated with its use.

Testing reveals bugs, but once discovered, bugs need to be repaired cleanly and correctly. Good design also involves designing systems that are more easily fixed when something goes wrong (a process often known as "anti-bugging"). For example, a well-designed system has clear documentation. Well-designed systems avoid hidden dependencies, so fixes at one point do not create new flaws at another. The system design itself facilitates examination of what the system is doing and enables the reporting of unexpected events.

Debugging also involves making the everyday elements of technology work. When something goes wrong, it is desirable to be able to trace the chain of events upon which correct operation depends. A typical example today starts with a person who tries to print a document prepared with a word processor, and the printer doesn't produce any output. There could be a flaw anywhere along a chain of potential causes: the printer isn't plugged in or is turned off; the printer isn't connected to the computer; the wrong driver is selected; the printer queue is blocked, improper parameters were set in the print command; and many other possible events. A user needs to recognize that this is a solvable problem, find the broken link in the chain, and either solve the problem or call the appropriate expert.

5. *Organize and navigate information structures and evaluate information.*

Most sustained activities involve the location, evaluation, use, and organization of information. Often searching for and locating information involve other aspects of FITness, including evaluating the validity of information and resolving conflicting accounts of situations. (Note also the connection to information literacy, discussed in Section 3.2.)

This capability also involves the ability to find and evaluate information at different levels of sophistication. Tasks range from reading a manual to finding and using online help. Web searches may be necessary to find more complex information. Of course, as the level of complexity rises, it becomes increasingly important (and more difficult) to ascertain accuracy. An individual must be prepared to evaluate the reliability of a source, understand the nature of a shared information space such as the Web, and regard with appropriate caution the quality of the information retrieved.

This capability also suggests that one must be able to structure information appropriately to make it useful. The information created must be retrievable and useful for the intended purpose. Thus, the design process for information structures involves elements of communication (and may involve programming of some sort).

6.   *Collaborate.*

When project responsibilities must be divided among a number of people, collaboration abilities are involved. Among other things, collaboration involves a strategy for dividing a task into pieces that can be worked on individually. In practice, how a problem is divided is based on both the structure of the problem and the organizational structure of the team that will solve it (e.g., different individuals may have different talents). In collaborating, individuals need to avoid duplication of effort as well as inconsistencies in the parts that they deliver for integration into the final product. Furthermore, each must have a clear sense for how the various parts of a solution are made to operate together as well as the expectations for his or her own part, the importance of clearly specified interfaces as a technique for increasing the likelihood that parts of a solution can operate together, and a strategy for ensuring that team members work on an appropriately recent version of the solution.

Information technologies used for collaboration do not change what is required of a collaboration, but they do change how a collaboration takes place. Information technologies such as telephones, e-mail, video-conferencing, shared Web pages, chat rooms, and so on enable collaborators to work together remotely and asynchronously, with relatively less reliance on face-to-face interactions. But learning how to cope with the limitations of technologically mediated interactions thus becomes essential. For example, if team members communicate by e-mail, they may well lose some ability to communicate clearly and unambiguously; at the very least, they may be forced to articulate things explicitly that a face-to-face interaction would not require.

7. *Communicate to other audiences.*

In conveying information to others, it is often necessary to use technology. This may involve the use of images or processes as well as words. Effective communication requires familiarity with and understanding of the pros and cons of various means of communication, because the intervening technology may change the nature of the communication. For example, it is much more difficult to provide driving directions to a given location by using the telephone than by gesturing and pointing to a map.

But a deeper aspect of communication with other audiences is the nature of that communication, independent of media. For example, communicating problem statements or project outcomes to customers, interested individuals, and others requires an understanding of audience needs and background knowledge. An effective communication to experts might involve translating informal needs into formal requirements, for example, moving from a "wish list" expressed during a lunchtime conversation to a more formal tasking to a work team. These formal requirements form the basis for discussing whether or not a project performs correctly, and therefore underlie the ability to test and debug. Without communication that carries nuance and detail, it is impossible to know whether a project component is being built correctly.

A related dimension of communication with other audiences is documentation. Documentation is almost always a component of informing an "outsider" audience about the nature of a system, such as an office system, a manufacturing system, or an information technology system. Documentation makes content more explicit and provides many opportunities for someone to think through the structure of a project. The development of documentation can be regarded as a process of devising the minimum set of information and instructions needed for an unknown task to be performed with a specific tool by a non-expert.

8. *Expect the unexpected.*

Even when a technological system works as intended to solve a problem as it was originally stated, its use may still have unexpected consequences, because the system is embedded in a larger social and technological context that may not have been properly anticipated. In some instances, these unexpected consequences may even overshadow the intended outcome (i.e., the solving of the original problem). Users should understand that such consequences are not uncommon and work to mitigate or exploit them as appropriate.

Unforeseen benefits or drawbacks may result when a technology deployed for one purpose is used for other purposes. For example:

- One of the original "primary" purposes of the ARPANET (the predecessor to the Internet) was to facilitate the use of computers many miles away from one's local desktop; as users learned how to use the ARPANET, they found that it was most useful for its e-mail capabilities.
- Making Web browsers in school libraries available to all students is intended to give students easy access to the rich information content of the Internet. But open access may unintentionally expose students to child molesters, hate speech, and pornography.

In other cases, unexpected side effects may occur because a technological system is deployed on a much larger scale than originally expected. For example:

- Introducing computers into schools on a large scale means that many teachers must be trained to use them effectively.[3]
- Introducing information technology into businesses on a large scale often results in unexpected recurring expenditures to keep hardware and software investments current with evolving applications.[4] Small applications of information technology can be funded on a shoestring (e.g., because problems can be solved in a "quick and dirty" manner). But on a large scale, maintenance, support, documentation, and training become big sources of expense.

Finally, technological systems may be designed for a particular intensity of usage, but may display unexpected behavior or may result in unexpected consequences when the actual intensity of usage is higher. For example:

- Acquisition of a cellular telephone "for emergency use only" for a low monthly payment often results in first-time bills that are much larger than expected, because the user finds the convenience of the cellular telephone irresistible.

---

[3]See, for example, Panel on Educational Technology. 1997. *Report to the President on the Use of Technology to Strengthen K-12 Education in the United States*, President's Committee of Advisors on Science and Technology (PCAST), Washington, D.C., March, Chapter 5.

[4]Such experiences in the private sector are often reported in the trade press. See, for example, M. Lynne Markus and Robert I. Benjamin. 1997. "Are You Gambling on a Magic Bullet?", *Computerworld*, October 20; Clayton M Christensen. 1997. "Fatal Attraction: The Dangers of Too Much Technology," *Computerworld*, June 16; Vaughan Merlyn and Sheila Smith. 1997. "Be Careful What You Wish For: Managing Technology's Unintended Consequences," *Computerworld*, January 20.

- A server designed for a particular load may crash when subject to too many requests for service arriving at the same time, as often happens when access is sought to a popular Web site.[5]

9. *Anticipate changing technologies.*

While no one can predict accurately the future course of technology, technology inevitably changes. FITness entails the capability to adapt to new technology efficiently and how to learn a new language or system, building on what is already known about older, perhaps similar technologies and facilities. For example, new versions of technology and tools will almost certainly appear, and they may offer benefits over older versions (e.g., the new version may be faster or offer more features). At the same time, additional functionality often comes at a cost (e.g., the need to upgrade system resources such as memory, or the need to learn the new set of features). Users thus must be prepared to weigh whether the benefits of the inevitable new version outweigh its costs. Decisions as to when or whether to upgrade, which tool to use, and how many features to learn are examples of such adaptation.

10. *Think about information technology abstractly.*

A person who effectively determines how to apply information technology to his or her needs will think about information technology abstractly. For example, she will reflect on her use of information technology, identifying characteristics and commonalities that cut across technological experiences. She will transfer the principles of technological solutions from one setting to another. She will recognize technological analogies, and use them to become adept with new technology quickly. She will have high expectations for technological solutions, and she will find work-arounds when technology falls short.

A second dimension of thinking abstractly about information technology is to consider what aspects of information technology affect a policy issue. For example, a person engaged in such thought will try to determine if and how the technology makes previous policy solutions inadequate. He or she will think deeply about proposed metaphors, such as assertions that putting up a Web page is equivalent to publishing.

---

[5]William Stallings. 1996. *Data and Computer Communications*, 5th Edition, Prentice-Hall, New York. See also Keynote Systems, Inc. 1998. "Top 10 Discoveries About the Internet," and "How Fast *Is* the Internet?" Available online at, respectively, <http://www.keynote.com/measures/top10.html> and <http://www.keynote.com/measures/howfast.html>.

2.5 INFORMATION TECHNOLOGY CONCEPTS[6]

If information technology were unchanging, then most people would find it unnecessary to learn information technology concepts. The information technology skills could be taught once and for all, and the conceptual foundation underlying information technology would be of interest only to specialists. But information technology changes daily and often dramatically, rendering present-day skills obsolete but also offering new opportunities to solve personally relevant problems. How can one prepare for this inevitable change? How can one quickly upgrade one's skills to exploit new opportunities?

The answer lies in understanding a few of the basic ideas and concepts underpinning information technology. These concepts are approximately independent of particular technology or applications, though they are instantiated in different ways in different technologies and applications. In particular, the new and improved information technology of the future will also depend on these concepts, and an understanding of the principles on which information technology rests will continue to enable a person to acquire information technology skills more easily. And, because these concepts are fundamental, they are far more enduring than information technology skills that are tied to specific technologies.

The topics given in the following list touch on ideas of computation, communication, and information that are deep and intellectually challenging. Although any of the topics could be the basis of years of graduate study for a specialist, the basic ideas are straightforward and accessible, having been regularly taught to nonspecialists for years. Note also that the time and effort required to teach and learn each concept may vary widely.

The concepts presented below reflect the committee's judgments about the most important conceptual foundations of information technology contributing to FITness. There is no intended order.

---

[6]The discussion in this section identifies various information technology concepts in a form that approximates that of a catalog description of a course. A full explanation of the concepts would be appropriate for a textbook, but not for a report attempting to outline a basic framework for understanding information technology. Some of these concepts may not be familiar to non-specialists, a point that previews a pedagogical approach discussed in Chapter 4 involving the joint teaching efforts of information technology specialists and domain experts.

1. *Computers*

    Key aspects of a stored-program computer, including:

    -   The program as a sequence of steps,
    -   The process of program interpretation,
    -   The memory as a repository for program and data (including notions of memory hierarchy and associated ideas of permanence/volatility), and
    -   Overall organization, including relationship to peripheral devices (e.g., I/O devices).

    The appropriate emphasis is not necessarily a specific electronic realization such as a particular computer, but rather the idea of a computational task as a discrete sequence of steps, the deterministic interpretation of instructions, instruction sequencing and control flow, and the distinction between name and value. Computers do what the program tells them to do given particular input, and if a computer exhibits a particular capability, it is because someone figured out how to break the task into a sequence of basic steps, i.e., how to program it.

2. *Information systems*

    The general structural features of an information system, including, among others, the hardware and software components, people and processes, interfaces (both technology interfaces and human-computer interfaces), databases, transactions, consistency, availability, persistent storage, archiving, audit trails, security and privacy and their technological underpinnings.

    Most knowledge workers in the labor force interact with one or more information systems, becoming knowledgeable about their characteristics and idiosyncrasies. Understanding the abstract structure of such systems prepares students for employment, enhances job mobility, enables workers to adapt to new systems more quickly, and helps them to exploit more fully the facilities of a given system.

3. *Networks*

    Key attributes and aspects of information networks, including their physical structure (messages, packets, switching, routing, addressing, congestion, local area networks (LANs), wide area networks (WANs), bandwidth, latency, point-to-point communication, multicast, broadcast, Ethernet, mobility), and logical structure (client/server, interfaces, layered protocols, standards, network services).

Computers are generally much more useful when connected to each other and to the Internet. The goal is to understand how computers can be connected to each other and to networks, and how information is routed between computers. The appropriate emphasis is how the parameters of communication, such as latency and bandwidth, affect the responsiveness of a network from a user's point of view and how they might limit one's ability to work.

4. *Digital representation of information*

The general concept of information encoding in binary form. Different information encodings: ASCII, digital sound, images, and video/movies. Topics such as precision, conversion and interoperability (e.g., of file formats), resolution, fidelity, transformation, compression, and encryption are related, as is standardization of representations to support communication.

The appropriate emphasis is the notion that information that is processed by computers and communication systems is represented by bits (i.e., binary digits). Such a representation is a uniform way for computers and communication systems to store and transmit all information; information can be synthesized without a master analog source simply by creating the bits and so can be used to produce everything from *Toy Story* animations to forged e-mail; symbolic information in machine-readable form is more easily searchable than physical information.

5. *Information organization*

The general concepts of information organization, including forms, structure, classification and indexing, searching and retrieving, assessing information quality, authoring and presentation, and citation. Search engines for text, images, video, audio.

Information in computers, databases, libraries, and elsewhere must be structured to be accessible and useful. How the data should be organized and indexed depends critically on how users will describe the information sought (and vice versa), and how completely that description can be specified. In addition to locating and structuring information, it is important to be able to judge the quality (accuracy, authoritativeness, and so forth) of information both stored and retrieved. Section 3.2 provides some additional discussion.

6. *Modeling and abstraction*

The general methods and techniques for representing real-world phenomena as computer models, first in appropriate forms such as systems of equations, graphs, and relationships, and then in appropriate programming objects such as arrays or lists or procedures. Topics include continuous and discrete models, discrete time, events, randomization, and convergence, as well as the use of abstraction to hide irrelevant detail.

Computers can be made to play chess, predict the weather, and simulate the crash of a sports car by abstracting real-world phenomena and manipulating those abstractions using transformations that duplicate or approximate the real-world processes. One goal is understanding the relationship between reality and its representation, including notions of approximation, validity, and limitations; i.e., not all aspects of the real world are modeled in any one program, and a model is not reality.

7. Algorithmic thinking and programming

The general concepts of algorithmic thinking, including functional decomposition, repetition (iteration and/or recursion), basic data organizations (record, array, list), generalization and parameterization, algorithm vs. program, top-down design, and refinement. Note also that some types of algorithmic thinking do not necessarily require the use or understanding of sophisticated mathematics. The role of programming, which is a specific instantiation of algorithmic thinking, is discussed in Chapter 3.

Algorithmic thinking is key to understanding many aspects of information technology. Specifically, it is essential to comprehending how and why information technology systems work as they do. To troubleshoot or debug a problem in an information technology system, application, or operation, it is essential to have some expectation of what the proper behavior should be, and how it might fail to be realized. Further, algorithmic thinking is key to applying information technology to other personally relevant situations.

8. Universality

The "universality of computers" is one of the fundamental facts of information technology discovered by computing pioneers A.M. Turing and Alonzo Church in the 1930s, before practical computers were created.[7] Shorn of its theoretical formalism and expressed informally, universality says that any computational task can be performed by any computer. The statement has several implications:

---

[7]Alonzo Church. 1936. "An Unsolvable Problem of Elementary Number Theory," *American Journal of Mathematics*, 58:345-363; Alan M. Turing. 1936. "On Computable Numbers, with an Application to the Entscheidungsproblem," *Proceedings of the London Mathematical Society*, Ser. 2, 42:230-265, 43:544-546.

- No computational task is so complex that it cannot be decomposed into instructions suitable for the most basic computer.
- The instruction repertoire of a computer is largely unimportant in terms of giving it power since any missing instruction types can be programmed using the instructions the machine does have.
- Computers differ by how quickly they solve a problem, not whether they can solve the problem.
- Programs, which direct the instruction-following components of a computer to realize a computation, are the key.

Universality distinguishes computers from other types of machines (Box 2.2).

9. *Limitations of information technology*

The general notions of complexity, growth rates, scale, tractability, decidability, and state explosion combine to express some of the limitations of information technology. Tangible connections should be made to applications, such as text search, sorting, scheduling, and debugging.

Computers possess no intuition, creativity, imagination, or magic. Though extraordinary in their scope and application, information technology systems cannot do everything. Some tasks, such as calculating the closing price for a given stock on the NASDAQ exchange, are not solvable by computer. Other tasks, such as that of placing objects into a container so as to maximize the number that can be stored within it (e.g., optimally filling boxcars, shipping containers, moving vans, or space shuttles), can be solved only for small problems but not for large ones or those of practical importance.[8] Some tasks are so easily solved that it hardly matters which solution is used. And, because the programs that run on computers are designed by human beings, they reflect the assumptions that their designers build into them, assumptions that may be inappropriate or wrong. Thus, for example, a computer simulation of some "real" phenomenon may or may not accurately reflect the underlying reality (and a naïve user may be unable to tell the difference between a generally true simulation and one that is fundamentally misleading). Assessing what

---

[8]In the case of the maximization problem above (often known as the "knapsack" problem), the proper arrangement can be determined by exhaustively trying all arrangements and orientations of the objects. But this calculation cannot be performed in any reasonable length of time when many objects can be placed into the container. Yet the penalty of not being able to find the maximizing arrangement can be high, as when shipping two containers rather than one or launching the Space Shuttle twice rather than once. When the problem is large enough that the maximizing arrangement cannot be practically computed, it is necessary to use "nearly maximal" arrangements that can be more easily determined.

Box 2.2
On Universality—In Principle and in Practice

The universality property of computers is a theoretical result. Is it true in practice? The answer is yes, definitely, but there are complicating practical issues that can obscure the truth of this fact.

How can a computer without connection to a printer perform the computation, "print the report"? Of course, it cannot. But, the computer can *without change* perform the task, given a printer and the necessary software to format the report and drive the printer. Similarly, a computer embedded in an automobile's carburetor cannot print a report either, because, first, it does not have the proper input/output devices and, second, its software is permanently set to the task of mixing fuel. But the computer, i.e., the central processing unit, is not a limitation in these or other cases. Indeed, it is the universality of computers that explains why they are so ubiquitous in modern America: a computer chip with a program stored in read-only memory (ROM) is more convenient to design, cheaper to build, more reliable, and easier to maintain than specialized circuitry for controlling appliances, automobile subsystems, and other mechanical devices, as well as electronics like cell phones and Global Positioning System (GPS) devices.

Further, the observation that applications like word processing require different software to run on a Macintosh versus a PC seems to contradict the above claims and imply that the instruction set does matter. In a narrow sense it does, since the Mac cannot directly execute the binary encoding of a program specialized to the PC and vice versa. This is because the Mac and the PC use different microprocessor chips and the binary files for software applications are customized for each type of microprocessor. But those two different binary encodings can be created from a single source program by a translator (compiler) that specializes the computation to each instruction set. The two machines are literally running the same source program, i.e., performing the same word processing computation. And there is an indirect sense in which any PC software can run on a Mac and vice versa. A program can be written for one machine to emulate the instruction set of the other machine, allowing it to execute the actual binary encoding used by the other machine. Being indirect, this would be slower than a customized version, but it truly illustrates universality.

information technology can be applied—and when it should be applied—is essential in today's information age.

10. *Societal impact of information and information technology*

The technical basis for social concerns about privacy, intellectual property, ownership, security, weak/strong encryption, inferences about personal characteristics based on electronic behavior such as monitoring Web sites visited, "netiquette," "spamming," and free speech in the Internet environment.

Understanding social issues strongly connected to information technology goes beyond FITness to general principles of good citizenship. Policy issues that relate to information technology, including privacy, encryption, copyright, and related concerns, are increasingly common today, and informed citizens must have a basis for understanding the significance of those issues and for making reasoned judgments about them.

Information technology connects to the world at large in many ways, and characteristics of the technology have implications for everyday issues. Consider, for example, intellectual property. Copyright is accompanied by a well-established body of law, but now that the Web makes images and documents available to a huge audience, it has become much more important for Web users to understand that the ability to see an image on the Web does not automatically imply that the image can be copied or reused.

Numerous other issues are apparent today on which many non-technologists are asked to make judgments. Is the Internet just another form of publication, and therefore subject to the same First Amendment and copyright protections that newspapers enjoy? Is encryption a potential weapon that needs to be kept out of foreign hands? Why are standards important, and how do we promote the use of standards without permitting unregulated monopolies to stifle innovation? Does inviting technologically skilled workers from other countries create or destroy jobs? How do we encourage children to achieve the highest levels of technological competence? Does information technology cause job displacement and/ or upskilling? How is it possible to promote social equity regarding access to information technology?

Discussion

These fundamental concepts represent major ideas underpinning information technology. The claim that FITness demands an understanding of these concepts is most frequently challenged by an analogy: If most people can drive without understanding how an automobile works, why should anyone need to know how a computer works?

The weakness in this analogy is embodied in the difference between the two kinds of machines. Automobiles perform essentially one task, transporting people and things from one location to another, and are incapable of other physical tasks, say, mixing concrete. Any computer can perform any information processing task—this is the concept of universality. It is not only a principle; it is a fact used every day. When one wants to manage a household budget, one doesn't buy a new computer for budgeting. Rather, one buys and installs software to add budgeting to the computer's other capabilities. Not being specialized like other machines that directly affect the physical world, computers may well affect our lives more than these other machines have, including automobiles. Knowing the conceptual foundations, then, is essential to understanding this impact—what information technology can do, what it cannot do, what risks computers and access to information bring, and so on. Armed with such knowledge, individuals can make informed choices ranging from personal decisions (like taking precautions against computer viruses) to matters of public policy such as protecting privacy interests.

An equally important motivation for learning information technology concepts is that they provide foundational knowledge to be used when acquiring and applying the intellectual capabilities. To perform the reasoning and thinking activities embodied in the capabilities, it is necessary to have some understanding of the range of possibilities. Furthermore, understanding these concepts enables an individual to be more versatile and more creative in his or her use of information technology tools.

Finally, Box 2.3 points out that even in a world in which the public's exposure to information technology is through specialized information appliances rather than desktop computers or through technologies that adapt to user needs and knowledge, the fundamental concepts of information technology will still be useful in understanding how to use such devices effectively.

2.6 INFORMATION TECHNOLOGY SKILLS

Skills such as managing a personal computer, using word processing, network browsers, mail, and spreadsheet software, or understanding an operating system are what are most usually subsumed under the label of "computer literacy."

Because information technology skills are closely tied to today's applications, the set of necessary skills can be expected to change at about the same rate that commercial information technology changes, i.e., quite rapidly. (Note, for example, that a list of skills developed five years ago would not have mentioned the Web or the Internet.) Changes in the specific interests and needs of the individual involved also have a significant effect on what skills are (or become) necessary. Over the course of a lifetime, individuals who use information technology must regularly evaluate their skills and determine which new skills they need for their workplace or personal success. FITness entails a continuing acquisition of new skills and adaptation of a set of skills to a changing environment.

The list of skills below is appropriate for today's technologies (circa

Box 2.3
FITness, Personal Computers, Information
Appliances, and Adaptive Technology

Today, desktop computers are a primary platform through which individuals interact with information technology. But whether this proposition will remain true in the future is an open question. Some reports suggest that information appliances—single-purpose devices that manipulate information—may become more common and ubiquitous in the future. Indeed, those making this prediction argue that information appliances can be made so easy to use that no knowledge of information technology will be necessary to operate them.

Predictions of the future technology environment are notoriously uncertain. It is likely that today's desktop computers (or their equivalents) will continue to be used by information workers. But the intellectual framework outlined in this chapter for FITness will continue to have applicability even to individuals dealing with information appliances. Of course, the specific skills needed will be different. But the basic concepts and intellectual capabilities of FITness will continue to be relevant. For example:

• An algorithm of some sort will be driving the operation of an information appliance. Understanding the general characteristics of algorithms will help the user to understand the limitations of a given device. For example, a navigation system for a car may provide the "best" route from Point A to B; the user may find it useful to know whether "best" refers to the most scenic route or the shortest route or the fastest route.

• Input to an information appliance is likely to remain "brittle," in the sense that the device will respond to the input that the user actually provides, not the input that the user intended to provide. This is a consequence of several concepts, including the digital representation of information and the nature of computational devices and information systems.

1999) and focuses on what one would need to know to buy a personal computer, set it up, use the principal software that comes with it, subscribe to an Internet service provider, and use its services. These items and other similar ones emerged from a question posed to attendees at the committee's January 1998 workshop about what an information technology-literate person should know.

This list of skills extends in one important way the content of "computer literacy" courses that teach individuals how to use specific software packages. It is true that students need to use specific software and hardware to acquire skills with information technology. But the skills involved in the committee's list are generic skills, rather than the specific skills

- A wireless information appliance that facilitates interaction with large amounts of data will require a local database for a fast response. The navigation system described above, for example, will in general not receive maps through the air, but rather will require maps "pre-stored" in some way that is local to the device.
- Identifying and correcting faults will always be necessary for the user to understand how he or she used the device improperly.

Furthermore, a knowledge of the basic concepts of FITness will enable a person to move more freely among information appliances. For example, a user will need to know to look for a way to correct mistaken input.

None of this is to argue the impossibility of operating an information appliance by the memorized application of a particular set of keystrokes—which today enables some individuals to obtain something useful from a computer. But gaining the full value from either a computer or an information appliance will require the full intellectual range of FITness.

In a similar vein, it can be argued that information technology should be—and someday will be—designed to minimize what the individual must know in order to use it. For example, some information technology applications attempt to adapt to a particular user's style and needs. Other applications attempt to conceal their internal operation to reduce the burden on the user.

Such technological adaptations to the relatively naïve user are unquestionably helpful. But they do not—indeed, cannot—eliminate the need for FITness. For example, it is hard to imagine that a complex application has no operating faults in it, and thus users will always have to cope with things that don't work. All of the rationales articulated above for FITness in the context of information appliances equally apply to well-engineered and user-adaptive information technology applications.

needed to operate a particular vendor's product. For example, "word processing" refers to the use of functionality common to most or all word processors, rather than the specific commands, key-bindings, or dialog boxes of one vendor's software. Acquiring these skills includes understanding what similarities and differences to expect between different products for the same task.

Today's set of ten essential skills includes:

1. *Setting up a personal computer*

   A person who uses computers should be able to connect the parts of a personal computer and its major peripherals (e.g., a printer). This entails knowing about the physical appearance of cables and ports, as well as having some understanding of how to configure the computer (e.g., knowing that most computers provide a way to set the system clock, or how to select a screen saver and why one may need to use a screen saver).

2. *Using basic operating system features*

Typical of today's operating system use is the ability to install new software, delete unwanted software, and invoke applications. There are many other skills that could reasonably be included in this category, such as the ability to find out from the operating system whether there is sufficient disk space.

3. *Using a word processor to create a text document*

Today, minimal skills in this area include the ability to select fonts, paginate, organize, and edit documents. Integration of image and other data is becoming essential. In the near future, requirements in this area will likely include the creation of Web pages using specialized authoring tools.

4. *Using a graphics and/or artwork package to create illustrations, slides, or other image-based expressions of ideas*

Today, this skill involves the ability to use the current generation of presentation software and graphics packages.

5. *Connecting a computer to a network*

Today, this process can be as simple as wiring the computer to a telephone jack and subscribing to an Internet service provider, although as more powerful communications options become available, this process may become more complex.

6. *Using the Internet to find information and resources*

Today, locating information on the Internet involves the use of browsers and search engines. The use of search engines and browsers requires an understanding of one's needs and how they relate to what is available and what can be found readily, as well as the ability to specify queries and evaluate the results.

7. *Using a computer to communicate with others*

Today, electronic mail is a primary mode of computer-based communication. Variants and improvements, as well as entirely new modes of communication, are expected in the future.

8. *Using a spreadsheet to model simple processes or financial tables*

This skill includes the ability to use standard spreadsheet systems and/or specialized packages (e.g., tax preparation software).

9. *Using a database system to set up and access useful information*

Today, SQL-based systems[9] are becoming ubiquitous in the workplace, and personal information managers are becoming increasingly common. In the future, different approaches, perhaps Web-oriented, may become the prevalent mode.

10. *Using instructional materials to learn how to use new applications or features*

This skill involves using online help files and reading and understanding printed manuals. One aspect of this process is obtaining details or features of systems one already comprehends; a second aspect is using the tutorial to grasp the essential models and ideas underlying a new system.

2.7   FITness IN PERSPECTIVE

The intellectual content of FITness is rich and deep. But the depth and richness of this content are determined by the nature of information technology. Although different individuals need different degrees of familiarity with the different elements of FITness, a good understanding of and facility with all of the skills, concepts, and capabilities of FITness are necessary for individuals to exploit the full power of information technology across a range of different applications.

Nevertheless, such depth and richness raise the question of the extent to which it is reasonable to expect that the content of FITness is accessible to a wide range of the citizenry. For perspective on this question, it is useful to consider the National Council of Teachers of Mathematics'

---

[9] SQL is an acronym for Structured Query Language, a common language used in interactions with databases.

(NCTM) standards for mathematics education and the National Research Council's standards for science education. As described in Appendix B, such organizations focus on the mathematical and scientific education of all students, rather than a special few with previously demonstrated aptitude for mathematics or science. The organizations that produced these standards for mathematics and science education make the case that the intellectual content articulated in the standards is rich, deep, and most importantly not "dumbed down." These organizations believe that learning about science and mathematics is valuable not just for future scientists and mathematicians, but also for a very wide range of the citizenry.

The essentials of FITness are not for the most part dependent on knowledge of sophisticated mathematics. Indeed, the capabilities and concepts, though not the skills, are intellectually accessible even without computers per se. For example, the concept of an algorithm can be expressed and conveyed in an entirely qualitative and non-mathematical manner even to a 4th grader by discussing the rules of a game or following a recipe in the kitchen. Thus, the committee believes that the intellectual content of FITness is no less accessible to citizens than the mathematics and science contained within the NCTM and NRC standards.

A second issue is the following: by design, FITness is a body of knowledge and understanding that enables individuals to use information technology effectively in a variety of different contexts. But does being FIT mean that one will never need to rely on an information technology expert? Put differently, does an individual's consultation of an information technology expert imply a lack of FITness for that individual?

There is certainly some level of FITness at which an individual will not need to rely on an expert to fix an information technology problem or to exploit a new opportunity offered by information technology. But even someone who is FIT enough to not have to rely on an expert may find it advantageous to do so anyway. For example, a highly FIT individual may simply decide that it is not worth his or her time to fix a problem, even if he or she could do so. Furthermore, even if an individual with more basic levels of FITness may still need to consult with an information techology expert to solve a technology problem or to describe a technology solution, that basic understanding and knowledge will help him or her to interact constructively with the expert (e.g., to recognize that a problem is indeed solvable; to explain the problem or solution requirements more precisely; or to understand, implement, or dispute an approach that the expert proposes).

3

Collateral Issues

Chapter 2 outlines an intellectual framework for FITness. But the specifics of the committee's articulation inevitably lead to concerns about two related issues. First, the role of programming as an essential element of understanding information technology is an issue that has been long debated in the computer science community. And, because the issue may seem like an esoteric diversion for the non-specialist, some words of explanation are appropriate. Second, for many years the library science community has promulgated the notion of information literacy. Because information literacy and fluency with information technology share certain elements, an explicit comparison between the two is warranted.

3.1 THE ROLE OF PROGRAMMING

Algorithmic thinking is a valuable ability for many educated people, yet programming—the act of expressing an algorithm in a specific form to solve a problem—is widely seen as the purview of the specialist. Algorithmic thinking and programming were listed together as a concept in Chapter 2, because they are very closely related forms of the same phenomenon. They are an implied constituent of many of the skills, concepts, and capabilities that embody the intellectual framework of FITness. This central role of programming coupled with the perception that it is the domain of experts mandates a careful explanation of what programming is and why it is so critical to FITness.

3.1.1   What Is Programming?

Many activities have been called programming, but not all of them meet the definition appropriate for FITness. For example, setting a video cassette recorder to tape an upcoming TV show is not programming, despite the fact that it has become a cultural icon for a technological task. Nor is scheduling the fall TV series programming as used here.

Programming, for the purposes of this report, is defined as the construction of a specification (sequence of instructions or program) for solving a problem by an agent other than the programmer. The action entails decomposing the problem into a sequence of steps and specifying them sufficiently precisely, unambiguously, and primitively that the interpreting agent, usually a computer, can effectively realize the intended solution.

Computer programming in a standard programming language meets this definition, of course, but programming arises in many other cases in which the agent is a human and the language is English. Giving directions to soccer players to find a particular field in a city, especially one not identifiable by numeric street/avenue coordinates, constitutes programming by this definition. A player is the agent interpreting or executing the instructions. Recipes with precise quantities of ingredients and precisely described preparation and cooking steps are programs executed by cooks. Toy manufactures write programs, called assembly instructions, for parents to follow, and the Internal Revenue Service (IRS) writes the program for "deductible IRA contributions" that taxpayers follow. (No comment is offered about the comprehensibility of such programs to an individual human being.)

Setting the VCR does not constitute programming by the foregoing definition, because only start/stop times, i.e., data, are being given. The data is input to a hard-wired program in the VCR. (This is parameter specification in technical terminology.) The situation does not call for the user to identify any sequence of steps. Using a phone menu is another instance of data presentation, though setting up the phone menu may constitute programming. One's ability to set a VCR, however, does benefit from using and understanding some of the FITness concepts and capabilities, e.g., dealing with unintended consequences, illustrating the point that components of FITness can translate to other technical settings.

Critical to the programming enterprise is specification that meets the conditions "precisely" and "primitively."

- "Precise" specifications are essential to provide assurance that the agent can determine which actions are to be performed and in what order, so that the intended result is achieved. Avoiding ambiguity is obviously crucial, but even seemingly unambiguous commands can fail. For example, "turn right" fails if the soccer players can approach the intersection from either the east or the west, so "turn north" is preferred. Similarly, "beat" and "fold in" are not synonyms for "stir" when combining ingredients, so successful recipes use precise terminology selected with great care. An important non-technology advantage of programming knowledge is that the need for precision can promote precision in everyday communication.

• "Primitive" specifications are essential to provide assurance that the steps to be performed are within the operational repertoire of the executing agent. The programmer may understand the task as "pi times R squared," but if the executing agent doesn't know what "squared" means or how to accomplish it, then the programmer must express the task in more primitive terms, perhaps revising it to "pi times R times R." For many taxpayers, the word "qualifying" in the IRS's instruction phrase "subtract qualifying contributions" would likely fail the test for primitiveness, because they would not readily understand what the term means.

Although programming can be as simple as giving a few commands—preheat oven to 350 degrees, combine dry ingredients, stir in eggs, press into greased loaf pan, bake for 20 minutes—most solutions require the use of conditional instructions and repetition of groups of instructions.

Conditional instructions are those that may or may not be performed, depending on the input to the program. This means that for different inputs, different sub-sequences of instructions will be performed. For example, in Box 3.1, the conditional instructions are presented for determining what happens in a baseball game when a batter walks. Programming with conditional instructions allows for solutions that can respond to different situations, leading to potentially more complex computations. Thus, one sequence of instructions is executed if there is a runner on first base, and a different sequence is executed if there is not.

Repeated instruction execution is a second essential programming construct, since it allows a program, for example, to process any number of data items rather than just a fixed number. Repetition is usually accomplished by enclosing processing instructions in a loop that repeats the processing until the data items are exhausted. Determining when the loop is completed requires a conditional test. Box 3.2 illustrates the use of iteration to calculate a batting average.

FITness-level programming experience implies facility with conditional instructions and repetition constructs. Though there are many types of instructions used by trained programmers, most are built on the

---

Box 3.1
Conditional Instructions for a Walk

The sentence shown in (a) is a specification in English of how the batter and runners advance when a batter walks in baseball. The indentations group the true and false alternatives of each conditional phrase. Though the solution in (a) is entirely satisfactory, a programmer would notice the redundancy of this direct solution and might reorganize it as shown in (b). The (b) solution tests for the presence of a runner on base and resolves that case, rather than treating the absence and presence of runners as separate cases. Notice that in program (b) a semicolon is used to separate consecutive statements, and parentheses have been added to assist in understanding the programmer's intent.

Solution (a)

If no runner is on 1st base then the batter goes to 1st base
otherwise there is a runner on 1st base, so
    if no runner is on 2nd base then the runner on 1st base
        goes to 2nd base and the batter goes to 1st base
    otherwise there are runners on 1st and 2nd, so
        if no runner is on 3rd base then the runner on 2nd base
            goes to 3rd, the runner on 1st goes to 2nd base
            and the batter goes to 1st base
        otherwise the bases are loaded, so
            the runner on 3rd goes home, the runner on
            2nd goes to 3rd, the runner on 1st goes to
            2nd, and the batter goes to 1st.

Solution (b)

If there is a runner on 1st base then,
    (if there is a runner on 2nd base then,
        (if there is a runner on 3rd base then
            the runner on 3rd goes home);
        the runner on 2nd goes to 3rd);
    the runner on 1st goes to 2nd);
the batter goes to 1st.

---

principles of conditional and/or repeated execution. In addition to experience with conditional and repetition constructs, FITness requires experience with at least two other fundamental programming ideas: functional decomposition and functional abstraction. These are the powerful mechanisms used by programmers to solve large problems (functional decom-

Box 3.2
Using Repeated Instruction Execution to Compute
DiMaggio's 1950 Batting Average

Figuring a batting average requires that the hits and times at bat for each game be accumulated, so a loop is used to consider the outcome of each game. The processing instructions are conditional on whether DiMaggio played in the game. The "game" is the data value that is changing with each iteration of the loop. Notice that this program assumes DiMaggio batted in at least one game in 1950.

Let the count_of_the_number_of_hits begin at 0.
Let the total_times_at_bat begin at 0.
For each game of the 1950 season beginning with the first,
    if DiMaggio played in the game then
        add DiMaggio's hits in this game to count_of_the_number_of_hits;
        add DiMaggio's times at bat in this game to total_times_at_bat;
DiMaggio's batting average is number_of_hits / total_times_at_bat.

position) and to reuse their earlier programming efforts (functional abstraction).

Finally, it is necessary to address the question of what programming language should be used to teach programming. This question has absorbed much energy of computer scientists, but the committee believes that while FITness does imply a basic programming ability, that ability need not be acquired in using a conventional programming language. For example, certain spreadsheet operations and advanced HTML programming for Web pages, among others, demand an understanding of enough programming concepts that they can provide this basic programming experience. Such applications will often yield more personally relevant opportunities to learn programming than programming in a conventional programming language.[1]

---

[1]And, programming has advanced significantly in recent years. Readers who may have been familiar with programming in the past, but have not stayed current, might be surprised to see how great has been the progress. Achievements such as object-oriented programming and program development environments have combined with graphical user interfaces and browsers to change a person's contact with programming in two significant ways. Furthermore, programming has been greatly simplified because of convenient access to a large reservoir of software. New scripting languages such as PERL, Java, and VBScript allow nonprofessionals to write modest programs that solve their problems.

This is not to say that the study of a conventional programming language cannot be sufficiently interesting, exciting, and rewarding for some students. But it is important to emphasize that being an accomplished programmer in a conventional programming language, e.g., C or Fortran or Java, is not sufficient by itself for FITness. Recognizing the centrality of programming, some traditional "information technology literacy" curricula have focused almost exclusively on programming in a conventional programming language. But programming cuts across the FITness spectrum, being essential to some aspects and nearly irrelevant to others.

3.1.2   The Importance of Programming Knowledge

The foregoing section outlines basic programming principles that are as fundamental to algorithmic thinking as multiplication and division are to mathematical thinking. Indeed, the parallel with mathematics is worth pursuing somewhat further.

At one time, arithmetic was considered the realm of specialists—reckoners—who were considered to have spiritual or magical powers.[2] Now, everyone learns arithmetic, calculators free us from the tedium of the actual symbol manipulation, and computers perform trillions of arithmetic operations per second. Educated people in industrialized societies give arithmetic little thought—it is an essential of modern life, a tool in their world of quantities.

Analogously, programming, the medium of algorithmic thinking, has traditionally been the realm of specialists. But, as is evident from the discussion above, programming principles are comprehensible and accessible. Universal knowledge of these principles is fundamental to an information society. To apply and exploit information processing technology that creates, manipulates, searches, and displays information, the population must be able to think algorithmically. As with arithmetic, the point is evident to those who think algorithmically, though it may be less obvious to those who do not yet do so.

How programming knowledge and experience can benefit one in an information society is made more explicit in the following three reasons for learning these concepts:

1. *Exploiting information technology systems.* Many prepackaged applications can be customized, extended, or enhanced using basic program-

---

[2]See, for example, Carl C. Boyer and Uta C. Merzbach, 1991, *A History of Mathematics,* John Wiley and Sons, New York, or Eric Temple Bell, 1991, *The Magic of Numbers,* Dover Publications, New York.

ming concepts. Serious use of spreadsheets requires programming, as does creating a sophisticated Web page. Furthermore, while not every personally relevant application will be available as prepackaged software, a person with a basic knowledge of programming may be able to "script" a solution using some of the large number of software building blocks now available commercially. Construction of complex systems from commercial software using macros, scripting facilities, shell commands, or other compositional tools is one way for non-specialists to use information technology in a personally relevant way.

Such activities constitute programming—developing a series of steps for an agent to solve a problem—where the "primitive operations" can be huge, e.g., whole database searches. In essence, this type of programming gives the non-specialist user the power to exploit tools fully and to transform computing resources so that they more completely meet their needs.

2. *Gaining knowledge assumed for capabilities.* Some of the capabilities that are at the heart of FITness rely explicitly or implicitly on programming knowledge. Thus, even if one does not expect to write programs, fully applying the capabilities requires some degree of familiarity with programming. For example, problems arise routinely in computing, even for the most casual computer user, so troubleshooting or "debugging" (a capability listed in Chapter 2) is needed. Yet, figuring out what device, system, or application is failing, and how, presumes at least rudimentary knowledge of how it is constructed and supposed to work. Rebooting the computer, restarting the application, or "jiggling" a connection may ultimately be necessary to solve a problem, but the need for such actions (and the likelihood that they may not solve the problem) can be reduced by understanding the algorithmic nature of the device or system and hence its possible failure modes Other capabilities that assume programming principles are those related to sustained reasoning and managing complexity.

3. *Application to non-information technology problems.* Since programming concepts arise in situations not related to information technology, formal instruction in information technology-related programming can be directly related to such problems. For example, returning to the situation of giving directions to a soccer field, a person who understands programming would likely provide directions that are independent of orientation, include "sentinels" of the form, "If you pass a church, you've gone too far," and are unambiguous, preferring "at the third light" rather than "after three lights." It hardly justifies studying programming, but it is a benefit. An example from an unexpected quarter: English professors

are authenticating Chaucer's tales using programs designed for testing DNA similarity that the professors modified to compare literary texts.[3]

In addition, the continual use of abstract thinking in programming can guide and discipline one's approach to problems in a way that has value well beyond the information technology-programming setting. In essence, programming becomes a laboratory for discussing and developing valuable life skills, as well as one element of the foundation for learning about other subjects.

For example, one difference between an algorithm and a program is that the algorithm embodies the basic structural features of the computation independently of the details of implementation, whereas a program commits to a specific set of details to solve a particular problem. Understanding this interrelationship is basic programming, but the principle applies throughout life, as the giving-directions example above suggests. One observes that a solution technique (corresponding to the algorithm) can be used in different problem situations (corresponding to the programs). Inversely, one expects that a successful problem solution embodies a more general process that is independent of the situational specifics. These observations are well-known life experience that most people actually acquire in daily life. But, these observations could be taught in the classroom, since programming provides both a concrete context for discussing the more general point, and a multitude of instances. This is an exciting possibility. Of course, there is no substitute for experience, but the ability to think abstractly, and to understand one's experience using abstractions, can be benefits that arise from an understanding of abstraction in programming.

3.2 THE RELATIONSHIP BETWEEN INFORMATION LITERACY AND FITness[4]

"Information literacy" is a term long used by the library science community to denote a competence to find, evaluate, and make use of infor-

---

[3]See Adrian C. Barbrook, Christopher J. Howe, Norman Blake, and Peter Robinson. 1998. "The Phylogeny of *The Canterbury Tales,*" *Nature,* August 27. Based on their adaptation and application of computerized techniques used by biologists to reconstruct evolutionary trees of different species from their DNA, the authors conclude that a number of neglected manuscripts of *The Canterbury Tales* are close descendants of Chaucer's original version, while many manuscripts often used by scholars are actually more distant relatives.

[4]This section is largely adapted (by permission) from Clifford Lynch, director, Coalition for Networked Information (CNI), "Information Literacy and Information Technology Literacy: New Components in the Curriculum for a Digital Culture," position paper submitted to the Committee on Information Technology Literacy, February 1998.

mation appropriately. Information literacy and FITness are interrelated but quite distinct. Information literacy focuses on content and communication: it encompasses authoring, information finding and organization, research, and information analysis, assessment, and evaluation. Content can take many forms: text, images, video, computer simulations, and multimedia interactive works. Content can also serve many purposes: news, art, entertainment, education, research and scholarship, advertising, politics, commerce, and documents and records that structure activities of everyday business and personal life. Information literacy subsumes but goes far beyond the traditional textual literacy that has been considered part of a basic education (the ability to read, write, and critically analyze various forms of primarily textual literary works or personal and business documents). By contrast, FITness focuses on a set of intellectual capabilities, conceptual knowledge, and contemporary skills associated with information technology.

Both information literacy and FITness are essential for individuals to use information technology effectively. Today, the acquisition and shaping of information are increasingly mediated by information technology. Information technology shapes the channels of publication, access, and dissemination of information. The nature of increasingly common digital documents raises new issues in the activities and practices of analysis, assessment, evaluation, and criticism. Much of today's information technology and supporting infrastructure is intended to enable communication, information finding, information access, and information delivery.

As it relates to FITness, information literacy implies that the skills and intellectual capabilities usually associated with traditional textual literacy—authoring and critical and analytic reading (including the assessment of purpose, bias, accuracy, and quality)—must be extended to the full range of visual (image and video) and multimedia communication genres. This includes an appreciation of interactive media, and also a recognition of the fluid nature of many digital forms, plus an understanding of the growing ability to use computers to edit or even fabricate what have traditionally been viewed as factual records of events (such as images).

Furthermore, as computer-based searching becomes increasingly central to information finding and research, FITness will require an understanding of how searching systems work, and of the interplay between indexing techniques, descriptive practices and organizational systems (cataloging, abstracting, indexing, rating), searching, and information accessibility, visibility, and impact. One important point is the limitations of both digital information resources (much material will not be available in digital form for the foreseeable future) and also of various searching techniques.

FITness also involves an understanding of information resources and how they are mapped into technological and economic structures, and how these resources interrelate. In essence, individuals need to form a conceptual map of information space. For example, they need to be guided in developing mental models of the relationships among documents on the Internet and in proprietary databases, library collections, and the like as a basis for learning to evaluate what information sources are likely to be most appropriate for their various information needs.

4

Implementation Considerations

4.1 IMPLEMENTATION IN PERSPECTIVE

Chapters 2 and 3 describe an intellectual framework for FITness. But while the committee believes that the framework of FITness is generally relevant to a very broad range of the citizenry, implementational issues are very different for every segment of the population that might benefit from FITness. As noted in the preface, issues of committee expertise and budget imposed some practical constraints, and the committee ultimately decided to restrict the *implementational* focus of the report to the higher-education community with which it was most familiar—the four-year college or university graduate. Box 4.1 offers a few comments on FITness and K-12 education.

A focus on college graduates is pragmatic as a first place to begin efforts to promote FITness:

• Efforts to promote FITness may be easier to implement in colleges and universities at first, compared to K-12 schools or settings outside educational institutions. A multitude of college-level models exist for promoting FITness, as described below. Furthermore, colleges and universities generally enjoy greater autonomy in changing curricula, as compared to K-12 schools (or school districts). And, they tend to have more computing infrastructure than K-12 schools and a greater ability to invest in more infrastructure.

• K-12 teachers are themselves schooled in colleges and universities. In the long run, FITness efforts that reach university graduates are an important enabler for efforts to promote such fluency among K-12 students.

51

Box 4.1
K-12 and FITness

Although the implementational focus of this report is primarily college and university education, a few comments about K-12 and FITness are appropriate.

First, the committee has described FITness as a continuum. The notion of a continuum is quite consistent with a powerful pedagogical approach in which an individual learns or covers the "same" material repeatedly, but from increasingly sophisticated perspectives that build on what has previously been learned. Thus, what a fourth grader learns in developing FITness is consistent with what he or she will learn in eighth grade, but in eighth grade the individual can bring to bear on his or her FITness efforts a broader range of experience and interests, as well as greater maturity, intellectual sophistication, and ability to abstract.

Second, what students can or should learn in college naturally depends on what they have learned prior to college. As efforts to promote FITness begin to take hold in the K-12 domain, colleges and universities will be able to make increasingly stronger assumptions about the level of preparation that entering students bring to such courses, in the form of information technology concepts and skills learned in secondary school or at home. Indeed, it may be that over time, some degree of FITness will become prerequisite knowledge required on entrance to college, like knowledge of algebra or a foreign language.

Third, the committee hopes that although it has produced a report that communicates most successfully to college and university faculty in disciplines other than those that traditionally make great use of information technology, the report will prove useful as a point of departure for the other audiences it would eventually wish to influence. It may well be that grade-appropriate efforts promoting FITness will be necessary (though not sufficient) for the success of efforts of K-12 educators to integrate information technology into K-12 education. Many of the issues faced in colleges and universities are similar to those faced in K-12 education as well. These include decisions about allocation of scarce technological resources, replacement cycles for machines, disposition of outmoded technology, rapid redesign of courses to incorporate new technological tools, and reassessment of instructional priorities based on technological innovation. In tackling the relatively simpler problems of content and pedagogy, the committee hopes that its work will provide an intellectually sound foundation upon which these other audiences can build their efforts.

Fourth, educational standards that focus on the acquisition of specific skills or recitation of specific concepts promote learning in isolation without any realizable connection to anything of interest to most individuals. Standards related to information technology revised to better reflect the integration of intellectual capabilities, fundamental concepts, and contemporary skills described in this report suggest a more holistic consideration based on the use of portfolios and other similar techniques.

• Future job growth is expected to be largest in those occupations requiring education beyond high school. Many of these jobs can be characterized as jobs for "knowledge workers," a very broad category of employment that is more likely to require the use of information technology.[1]

A final reason for emphasizing college and university efforts is to promote equity. In an ideal world, all students would have access to the technological resources necessary to support their personal and professional interests. But in reality, technological advances frequently leave behind individuals with few opportunities, resources, wealth, or access to public facilities.[2] Colleges and universities provide important opportunities for such individuals, and such opportunities can be used to break down barriers to education, knowledge, and power. Conscious efforts to attack disparities in preparation among incoming students may well be necessary to promote a goal of all students graduating more FIT.

Enhancing undergraduate education for FITness will not be easy. U.S. undergraduate education is challenged as never before. Access to knowledge has become a requirement for many decent jobs, while at the same time, students, parents, administrators, and public officials look with dismay at the prospect of longer and more expensive courses of study required for a four-year baccalaureate degree. Solving the problem with ever-more narrow disciplines whose graduates know more and more about less and less is unsatisfactory. Such segmentation poorly serves a world where career changes are frequent and cross-disciplinary communication is needed to solve systemic problems.

The committee has considered the challenge of undergraduate education in two ways. First, its definition of FITness is parsimonious, broad, and flexible, with only ten requirements each in the three types of knowledge: capabilities, concepts, and skills. How the importance and context

---

[1]See, for example, George T. Silvestri. 1997. "Occupational Employment Projections to 2006," *Monthly Labor Review*, 120(11).

[2]For example, a report by the National Telecommunications and Information Administration (NTIA) found, based on census data, that while as a whole the United States has achieved a significant increase in the last several years (i.e., between 1994 and 1997) in its ownership of computers and modems and its use of e-mail, the growth favors certain groups over others, and furthermore the gap between these groups is increasing over time. For example, those living in central cities and rural areas lag behind the national average for computer ownership and online access. Income levels, race, and educational levels greatly affect penetration levels. Nationally, the "least connected" groups are the rural poor, rural and central city minorities, young households, and female-headed households. See NTIA. 1998. *Falling Through the Net II: New Data on the Digital Divide*, Washington, D.C. Available online from <http://ntia.doc.gov/ntiahome/net2/falling.htm>.

for each of these 30 requirements are tailored to the career and intellectual interests of individual students is the focus of this chapter. Second, it recognizes the practical issues of introducing new content into under-graduate curricula that are already packed.

4.2 A PROJECT-BASED APPROACH TO DEVELOPING FITness

Although the content of FITness is presented in Chapter 2 as a list of items, such a characterization does not imply that lecturing about them is the optimal form of instruction. FITness is fundamentally integrative, requiring the coordination of information and skills with respect to multiple dimensions of a problem and the need for making overall judgments and decisions taking all such information into account. For this reason, the committee believes the best way to develop FITness is through project-based education. Projects weave together the skills, concepts, and capabilities of FITness to achieve a tangible result. In a project, specific information technologies will be used, motivating students to become skillful with such things as databases, e-mail, and presentation software. Understanding the range of alternatives and implementing the solution will rely on or motivate learning the underlying concepts.

Projects of appropriate scale and scope inherently involve multiple iterations that provide opportunities for instructional checkpoints or interventions. And, an appropriately scoped project will be sufficiently complex that intellectual integration is necessary to complete it. (Appendix A provides some illustrative projects.)

An appropriately scoped project demands collaborative efforts. Project-based collaborative efforts are pedagogically valuable for several reasons. First, developing true expertise in any area requires the individual involved to assume a variety of different roles—creator, critic, partner, supporter, and so on—and a collaborative group effort is a natural setting in which to exercise these roles. Furthermore, learning to specialize and to deliver one's special information to a group is an important dimension of developing expertise, and so project-based learning helps teach students the character and nature of varied roles as well as how to play the role of a specialist. Second, a project requiring multiple collaborators can be large and complex enough to raise important intellectual and strategic issues that simply do not arise when problems are artificially delimited to be completely doable by a single individual. Third, students benefit from hearing explanations formulated by peers as well as experts.[3]

---

[3]The literature on collaborative learning is extensive. See, for example, Gavriel Salomon (editor). 1993. *Distributed Cognitions: Psychological and Educational Considerations: Learning in*

A project-based approach is consistent with many different instructional models:

• *Instruction as transmission of information.* In this model, lectures, books, and other materials transmit the information that students need to learn.

• *Instruction as active learning.* This model suggests that students learn best by actively engaging the material through asking questions, answering questions, pushing buttons, doing experiments, or using tutoring programs.

• *Instruction through discovery learning.* In discovery learning, students learn with little direct guidance on the theory that students who "discover" solutions on their own will be more likely to remember and master the competency and be able to apply that competency in like situations. Students who are spoon-fed will frequently not develop the cognitive maps associated with real mastery.

Each of these models can support project-based learning, though in practice no one approach suffices for a successful project. Effective courses need support and scaffolding so individuals can test their understanding against expectations regularly and obtain feedback on their weaknesses.

No single project bestows FITness, but a series of well-chosen projects can provide a foundation for the lifelong journey toward FITness. By working on a number of projects, students will have opportunities to use similar principles of technological solutions in different settings, to recognize technological analogies, to develop reasonable expectations for technological solutions, and to find work-arounds when technology falls short. A series of projects can provide sufficient breadth and diversity of experience that students can realistically "learn the rest" on their own, thus providing the intellectual foundation for self-directed, lifelong learning that can occur in many non-classroom settings.[4]

Doing—Social, Cognitive, and Computational Perspectives, Cambridge University Press, New York. A piece by Roy Pea, "Practices of Distributed Intelligence and Designs for Education," in this volume is particularly compelling.

[4]While lifelong efforts to develop and maintain FITness depend most importantly on an adequate intellectual foundation, other elements are important as well. For example, students often lose access upon graduation to the information technology infrastructure they used to develop FITness. They may regain some level of access when they take new jobs, but the new information technology infrastructure may well not be as sophisticated as that left behind, disadvantaging them in subsequent efforts to maintain FITness. Some universities now offer graduates access to some basic facilities, such as "e-mail for life"; these steps move in the right direction. Of course, individuals must do their part as well, such as obtaining access to a computer that provides them with access to the infrastructure.

Undertaking projects in complex problem domains provides a natural context in which FITness can be developed. For effective pedagogy, problem domains must be personally relevant so that the learner has reason to revisit and redefine his or her understanding of information technology. Individuals must use information technology in a domain they understand in order to develop FITness, but as long as that domain is relevant to the individual, it does not matter which domain is involved.

Finally, the description of capabilities, concepts, and skills described in Chapter 2 naturally raises for many educators the question of how much time is needed for each capability, concept, and skill in a time-limited curriculum for students to promote FITness. However, because FITness is a continuum, a specific educational context is needed to answer this question concretely. A course promoting FITness for history majors may well have a different weighting of topics than a course promoting FITness for engineers. A mini-course taught in an "independent activities period" designed for first-year students without designated majors is certain to be structured differently than a two-semester course for graduating seniors. Such matters are best handled by those who know the resource constraints of time and the availability of computing resources, as well as the competing needs, how the knowledge and skills are likely to be applied, and the value of deeper understanding to other student objectives.

The treatment of the three components of FITness—skills, concepts, and capabilities—may be approached differently. Students can learn word processing through the need to prepare and submit essays, spreadsheets or databases through the need to manipulate data in science courses, and so on. Many students will develop some of these skills prior to college, but even those who do not will have considerable motivation to learn them. College students have many non-curricular opportunities to develop current information technology skills, such as reading self-instruction books, learning from friends, or taking college or university workshops and non-credit courses taught by non-faculty professionals, e.g., computing center professionals and librarians.

The fundamental concepts are somewhat harder to integrate into standard curricula. However, as instructors develop and structure their courses to use information technology for enhanced pedagogical effectiveness, it will be increasingly possible to take advantage of the opportunities thereby provided for discussing the fundamental concepts and the application of these concepts in terms that are relevant to the disciplinary content of those courses. For example, art students study images, and often these images are images on a computer screen. But understanding the fidelity of these images to the originals requires an understanding of how images can be digitally represented. A business course might use computer simulations to demonstrate business processes. But understanding the limitations of a simulation requires understanding how processes can be modeled and the nature and scope of their limitations.

The capabilities also warrant being taught as part of disciplinary or departmental instructional programs. Indeed, these capabilities contribute both to FITness and to developing analytical skills that are necessary for success in multiple disciplines. The mode of instruction is primarily through projects that serve the purposes of the domain yet offer students the opportunity to learn and/or exercise the ten capabilities.

4.3 INFUSING FITness INTO THE UNIVERSITY

Many, if not most, colleges and universities understand that information technology will play an increasingly large role on their campuses.[5] Indeed, some are requiring that all matriculating students have a personal computer for use throughout their college careers. Some courses are being restructured and some new curricula are being developed to take advantage of new pedagogical opportunities offered by information technology.

Students who are successful in these courses must have skills adequate to support their use of the technology, and most institutions and courses provide some opportunities—whether in for-credit courses or not—for students to learn these skills. But the fundamental concepts and intellectual capabilities do not seem to be essential in these courses in any meaningful way. The challenge for colleges and universities is then how to build on the existing infrastructure of hardware, support services, and technology-adapted curricula and courses to support FITness.

One common reaction to calls for proficiency in X is to promulgate required courses on X. For example, in response to concerns about the writing ability of students, many universities require all students to enroll in (or place out of) a writing course. Only rarely have calls for new, universal courses of this type had a significant impact on curricula. Nevertheless, one first step toward FITness is a single college course, open to all students. No one course can fully realize the power and breadth of FITness, but it can provide a solid foundation upon which an individual can build further knowledge independently. With such a foundation in place, pedagogical efforts involving information technology should be easier and more efficient to undertake in subsequent courses.

This college-wide course would require students to complete a series

---

[5]See, for example, "Computers Across Campus," *Communications of the ACM*, January 1998, pp. 22-25.

of projects as a medium for acquiring the FITness capabilities and simultaneously to develop their understanding of the concepts and skills of FITness. It would be laboratory-intensive and ideally would draw projects from subject disciplines in which the student had some expertise or interest, whether or not those disciplines were technical. Thus, disciplines from engineering to economics or art history would be fair game.

If such a course were added to the undergraduate curriculum, what might it replace? The answer to this question will vary from one institution to the next, and there are a number of alternative strategies. For instance, many colleges and universities now offer a conventional computer literacy course for nonmajors, taught by the computer science faculty. It usually covers many of the topics listed as skills and concepts under FITness. In some cases, it also covers some of the capabilities by way of a programming laboratory component. This course could be converted, or updated, so that students who complete it are more FIT.

A better approach to FITness draws on the idea that information technology is pervasive. That is, when properly integrated, FITness will benefit the study of any subject, much as the ability to write well benefits students of any subject. By analogy to efforts that promote "writing in the major field of study," universities might consider offering FITness courses within a home discipline that are team-taught with a faculty member from the home discipline (who would provide the disciplinary context) and a faculty member from computer science (who would provide the conceptual foundations for information technology).[6] For instance, a FITness course team-taught by a computer scientist and an economist might involve projects in which students would apply algorithmic problem-solving skills to the development and exercising of economic models using appropriate modeling software. Science and engineering majors might benefit from a more thorough study of computer modeling, while humanities majors might benefit from a more thorough study of locating and evaluating information. Box 4.2 provides some examples of disciplinary courses that help to promote some aspects of FITness.

Over time, a series of these initiatives can help an institution educate graduates with a considerable measure of FITness, regardless of their major field of study. In the long run, faculty in various subject areas would offer courses that allow students to develop further their mastery of the concepts, skills, and capabilities of FITness in the context of problems drawn from their own fields; such courses would build on the foun-

---

[6]Because the concepts of information technology may be harder to teach in the context of other subject material (especially non-technical subject material), pairing a computer scientist with a faculty member in a home discipline may be particularly advantageous for explicating the fundamental concepts of information technology in a context that is relevant to the home discipline.

dations of FITness established in earlier years. Experience in establishing departmentally based efforts to fulfill global university-wide requirements (e.g., in areas such as expository writing) provides some confidence that departments can be successful in supporting university-wide goals to promote FITness.

Even apart from discipline-oriented courses, other instructional venues offer opportunities to develop FITness. Most institutions acknowledge that information technology will play an increasingly important role on their campuses. Thus, with information technology an increasing presence on campuses, most course designers make decisions (even if only implicitly) about what role information technology will play in their courses, e.g., whether students can communicate with the instructor electronically, are allowed to submit handwritten rather than typed papers, or are able to access the syllabus or homework assignments online. In addition, the institution itself provides many opportunities for using technology—course registration, class participation (e.g., through chat rooms), tutoring, application for financial aid, homework submission, databases of campus event information, and library research are among the possibilities.

Lest the integration of FITness across the curriculum appear too simple, the committee reminds the reader that a successful implementation of FITness instruction requires serious rethinking of the curriculum, just as campus-wide efforts to improve the writing abilities of undergraduates have involved such rethinking. The greatest successes in these latter efforts have been achieved not through a mandated requirement that all students complete the same writing course, but rather through the integration of writing into the fabric of courses taken by disciplinary majors.

Although Box 4.2 provides examples of individual courses that incorporate elements of FITness, projects that involve information technology in some essential way are still rare in non-technical courses. Universities need to concern themselves with the FITness of students who cross discipline boundaries and with the extent to which each discipline is meeting the goals of universal FITness.[7] The broad university-wide challenge is less about those disciplines where technology is stereotypically included (e.g., engineering) than those where technology is stereotypically rel-

---

[7]The difficulties of promulgating large-scale change across an entire curriculum are well documented. For example, many analysts believe that a faculty reward system that actively discourages junior faculty from developing innovative courses (because such work takes time away from research and publishing efforts) is a major impediment to change (see, for example, National Research Council, 1999, *Information Technology and the Transformation of Undergraduate Education*, National Academy Press, Washington, D.C.). But these issues are beyond the scope of this report.

Box 4.2
Multiple Routes for Developing Aspects of Fitness

FITness can be developed in a wide variety of venues. Consider the following courses:

• Students in the social sciences and humanities and in the professional schools other than engineering at Berkeley can take an introductory interdepartmental course on information technology that deals with the conceptual foundations of computing and information technology, the structure and function of computing systems, elements of programming, and applications programs. Course examples are drawn mainly from word processing, database management, electronic spreadsheets, graphics and simulation, and telecommunication.

• Sociology students at Bowdoin College can take a social research course that provides firsthand experience with the specific procedures through which social science knowledge is developed. The course emphasizes the interaction between theory and research, and includes field and laboratory exercises that involve observation, interviewing, use of available data (e.g., historical documents, statistical archives, computerized data banks, cultural artifacts), sampling, coding, use of computers, and elementary data analysis and interpretation.

• Students at Stanford University can take a variety of short, for-credit courses on the basics of computing. Subjects include word processing, spreadsheets, using UNIX, using the World Wide Web, and using university resources. Additional subjects include Web authoring tools, programming in specific languages such as Java or C++, problem solving with Mathematica, and security and privacy issues.

• Public policy students at Johns Hopkins University can take a course on the tools and techniques of policy implementation, including selecting strategies, weighing alternatives, and planning for contingencies; preparing budgets, which are the heart of public programs, and developing schedules

egated to a minor role or no role at all (e.g., the humanities[8]). Thus, it is not sufficient for individual instructors to revisit their course content or approach. As with the efforts to promote writing, campus-wide collaboration is needed to develop appropriate goals for FITness and to determine how departments will contribute to those goals, and in any event,

---

[8]See, for example, American Council of Learned Societies. 1998. Occasional Paper No. 41, "Computing and the Humanities: Summary of a Roundtable Meeting." Available online from <http://www.acls.org/op41-toc.htm>.

that ensure that plans are realized; recruiting and keeping a winning staff; and making a cogent and persuasive presentation. Students are expected to use technology to carry out the assignments, including the use of PowerPoint for their presentations and spreadsheets for their budgets. A portion of the course is specifically devoted to developing and managing data systems.

- Students at Carnegie Mellon University design and implement a history database to answer complex questions in history. They frequently draw on the Great American History Machine (a historical geographical database) to carry out their more limited database designs.[1]

- Students in introductory economics courses at a number of different institutes use Excel or STELLA to create a model of an economic problem or historical event and demonstrate the factors contributing to the outcome. Students typically predict what they think an appropriate model will be and then refine it when they find out that it is not adequate or complete.

- Students design artistic animations using complex three-dimensional modeling tools in some courses at the University of Illinois. Students in these courses typically have majors in art, art history, and computer graphics. Often joint projects involve individuals interested in becoming artists and individuals with expertise in computer science.

- In physiology courses, for example at the University of California, students use STELLA and related tools to design models of human systems, such as the renal system. Undergraduate students each devise models for parts of the renal system and then connect them to represent the entire human renal system.

---

[1]See, for example, John Modell and David Miller. 1998. "Teaching United States History with the Great American History Machine," *Historical Methods*, 21(3):121-134.

the process through which FITness can become a part of the regular curriculum must be evolutionary.

Faculty development is an essential dimension of campus-wide preparation to promote FITness. That is, to offer courses that seriously integrate appropriate information technology concepts, skills, and capabilities, instructors themselves will need to learn and utilize effectively the appropriate technologies as they become available for teaching and research in their respective disciplines. For instance, many fields within the social sciences are beginning to use computational-modeling software

---

Box 4.3
**Imperatives for Universities in Adopting Information Technology
for Instructional Purposes**

Improving Teaching and Learning

• Develop a coordinated, cross-departmental organization to advance the institution's goals in instructional technology.
• Equip more classrooms with basic and advanced information infrastructure.
• Provide better and more extensive training and support services in pedagogy and multimedia technology.
• Expand the availability of software site licenses, including better tools for building instructional materials.
• Create new, flexible multimedia learning environments.

Supporting Students

• Develop programs to ensure universal individual student access to (ownership of) network-enabled computers.
• Provide basic universal competency training in the use of online information resources for all students who do not yet have it.
• Provide more extensive and readily available help-desk facilities for students and faculty.
• Expand and modernize drop-in facilities with a mix of multimedia development capabilities, docking stations, printers, advanced software, and so on, with consulting support.
• Enhance the capabilities of universal e-mail and provide voice mail.

---

to help exercise and explain the principles of various social science phenomena, such as population growth or the interactions between various elements of the economy. Nevertheless, universal faculty FITness is not a prerequisite for universal student FITness, and not every course in a discipline needs to have a FITness component.

Currently, the level of FITness among college and university faculty is uneven, both among the disciplines and within any single discipline. For faculty who accept the idea that FITness is both fundamental to their students' mastery of their discipline and to their academic careers, support for faculty and curriculum development is necessary to help them become more FIT. Initially, such support might be external (e.g., provided by foundations), but over time, the institutions themselves must be willing to make the necessary investment on an ongoing basis. Evolution

• Provide facilities for universal Web publishing for students and student organizations, and consistent home pages for all courses.

• Develop capabilities to demonstrate, and to lend where appropriate, advanced tools and unique resources to students.

• Improve online student access to enrollment, financial, and advising information.

Improving Access to Library Resources

• Expand the availability of digital resources such as subscriptions to journals, digitized museum collections, and others.

• Provide electronic course reserves and enhanced digital reference materials.

• Expand and modernize workstations for access to information resources throughout the library.

Improving Network Infrastructure

• Expand the bandwidth of the campus digital network, the backbone and nervous system of the electronic dimension of the university.

• Complete network connectivity to all residential living facilities.

• Provide affordable off-campus access to the institution's network and the Internet.

• Expand video delivery capabilities throughout the campus.

SOURCE: Adapted from "Improving Instructional Technology at the University of California, Berkeley," Campus Computing and Communications Policy Board, Subcommittee on Instructional Technology, October 18, 1996. Available online at <http://socrates.berkeley.edu/~cccpb-it/ITReport10 18-96 html>

will also play a role in faculty development, in the sense that as new faculty are hired they will bring to the institution new expectations for information technology support, both in their research and in their teaching.

Curricular change will unfold in a context of broad integration of information technology into most aspects of a university operation and function in which instructors and administrators deploy the technology to support such possibilities (and associated infrastructure, such as adequate bandwidth for student usage) and learn how best to use that technology. For most students, the effectiveness with which they can use the university's information infrastructure will to a great extent determine the value of their educational experience. Box 4.3 describes some institutional imperatives for enhancing instructional use of information technology that will also support FITness.

Appendixes

APPENDIX
A

Illustrative Projects

The example projects in this appendix are described with different levels of detail and different emphases, as one would expect from projects conceptualized by individuals from different disciplines. These diverse projects are intended to demonstrate that projects dealing with different domain areas can all support efforts to develop fluency with information technology (FITness).

A.1 DEVELOPING A BUSINESS PLAN FOR A COMPUTER STORE

Module Placement: A course in business administration, computer science, applied mathematics

Task: Develop a business plan for a computer software and hardware store in a mall. To carry out this project, students should do the following:

- Decide on products to sell,
- Develop a pricing strategy,
- Consider staffing issues,
- Devise a marketing approach,
- Create an inventory policy,
- Design the store, and
- Make a presentation to the bank and mall representatives.

All of this should be discussed in the business plan.

Delivery: A CD-ROM or Web site providing a project scenario electronically

Background: A shopping mall would like to fill a commercial opening with a computer store. Teams of four should apply for the space by creating a business plan that could be used to apply for a bank loan. The bank, which has financed most of the mall, will select the applicants who present the best business plan. The store's emphasis will be on selling to first-time buyers looking for a computer for their home or for a very small business.

Project Add-ons: Students could also consider possible changes to their product line as new technologies become available.

Pedagogy: Students will work in teams of four. The project will extend over a period of approximately eight to ten weeks, with the final week devoted to student reflection on lessons learned and possible applications to other business ventures. Students will use technology in the design process: e.g., word-processing and presentation software, e-mail, the World Wide Web, spreadsheets, and even computer-aided design and manufacturing tools to design the store. Milestones should be established for each task of the project.

A.2   DESIGNING AN HIV-TRACKING SYSTEM FOR A HOSPITAL

Module Placement: A course in computer science, health administration, or biology (immunology, epidemiology)

Task: Design an information system to track HIV infections for a community hospital and its outreach clinics. The project should identify necessary:

- Hardware—equipment to run the system;
- Software—tracking expenditures, patient information;
- People—staffing requirements; and
- Processes—implementation schedule, staff training sessions, written report, and oral presentation.

Delivery: A CD-ROM or Web site providing a project scenario electronically

Background: The community hospital is running education, prevention, and treatment programs for HIV (and maybe other sexually transmitted diseases). The community health director wants to evaluate the three programs continuously so that he/she can make them more cost-effective while reducing the incidence of HIV in the community. Decisions include allocation of financial and staff resources among and within the three programs. A variety of individuals express concern about various aspects of the different programs, including issues of equity, confidentiality, and "family values" (education and sexual activity). Students should be given data on community size, current case loads, and so on. Students' written report should include a budget, staffing requirements, and implementation schedule, including specifications for staff training. Students should also make a presentation to the hospital board; ideally the latter would include representatives from a local hospital, a school of public health, and a private computer science firm.

Project Add-ons: Students should research and recommend security and privacy measures for the program

Pedagogy: Students will use technology in the design process: e.g., word-processing and presentation software, e-mail, the World Wide Web, spreadsheets, system design (flow chart) software, and databases. Milestones should be established for each task of the project.

A.3 DESIGNING AND IMPLEMENTING A CLIENT MANAGER DATABASE

Module Placement: A course in business, management, non-profit administration

Task: Complete a simple yet useful database that has been started by teaching assistants. The work will focus on the user interface aspect of the system. Design the final product to be a visually attractive database that a bank could use to keep track of clients and their accounts.
The user of the system should be able to:

- View a client's entire record,
- View all clients in list form,
- Find and view the bank's top clients,
- Sort based on multiple criteria, and
- Print mailing labels for all of the clients or for a user-defined subset.

Delivery: A client manager database

Background: Databases are a useful way of storing related information. They simplify organization and retrieval of the data and become more powerful and useful as data sets grow larger. With the rapid growth of information and the proliferation of the Internet, databases will become an even more important part of day-to-day life. One of the main parts of this assignment will be to create an attractive, consistent, and intuitive user interface. An example of a successful user interface should be provided to students. Besides designing the user interface, students will also be doing other database tasks, such as designing layouts, creating fields, writing simple scripts, and working with queries and sorts.

Teaching assistants should begin the project and provide a database shell, which includes the following information:

- Some of the fields, preconfigured, that the database relies on;
- Both fully completed layouts and partially completed ones to get students started;
- Script stubs, so that students need only complete the meaningful part of the scripts;
- Buttons that have already been linked to their associated scripts; and
- A rich user interface that includes buttons, icons, and background colors, and that serves to integrate the layouts in the database.

The shell should be designed to allow students to focus on the meaningful and important aspects of the assignment.

Each record will store the:

- Client's name,
- Client's address,
- Several means of contact with the client,
- Assets in several different accounts, and
- Free-form notes.

Data entry will be facilitated by pop-up menus.

Students are responsible for:

- Creating some additional fields,
- Updating two existing layouts and creating an entirely new one,

- Filling in several scripts that facilitate movement between different parts of the database,
    - Providing a simple sorting facility for the user, and
    - Entering some sample data (to help test the assignment).

Project Add-ons: There is significant opportunity for extra credit in this assignment. For example, try implementing one or more of the following features:

- Set up a mail merge that uses information from records in the database.
    - Write other useful and more complicated scripts.
    - Incorporate multimedia (such as pictures, video).

Pedagogy: This project seeks to familiarize students with databases through design and implementation that emphasize designing a quality user interface and learning to program in a simple scripting language.

A.4 DESIGNING AND IMPLEMENTING A SPREADSHEET-BASED HOME BUDGET

Module Placement: A course in computer science, library science, liberal arts

Task: Create a home budget that a typical family could use to track their income and expenditures over the course of a year. To accomplish this task, create a system of linked spreadsheets in Microsoft Excel that will help organize and process this information.

Delivery: A spreadsheet-based home budget software program

Background: The system should consist of a single workbook and must have the following properties and features:

- Tracking for six classes of expenses; examples include food, housing, automobile expenses, movie rentals, and so on.
- Income tracking, including monthly, weekly, or biweekly salary, taxes, and miscellaneous income. A summary of this data should be provided as well.
- Tracking for multiple bank accounts, with the ability to note account transactions (withdrawals and deposits). The balance for each account should compute automatically depending on the transactions, in-

cluding a simple interest calculation, so that the user only needs to enter a starting balance to begin using the account tracking system.

• Summary of total expenses and income, by month. This should also include a graphical representation of the summary, and a three-dimensional graph that displays all expenses, by month (note that there should be three separate axes).

Students are free to determine a design for the spreadsheets. There is no "one right way" to do it. The workbook should be logically organized and well formatted to give it a consistent and attractive appearance. Students should become familiar with spreadsheet concepts—through lectures, manuals, or online tutorials and help. (Teaching assistants could develop an Excel tutorial.)

Students should consider sketching the system design on paper before beginning to develop it electronically. Such a design should include how to divide the information into separate spreadsheets, how to link data from separate sheets, and what graphs to provide to help the user analyze the underlying data. Students should also concentrate on the work of calculating and linking the data before tackling the formatting and visual appeal of the spreadsheet. This approach encourages focusing on getting the basic structure of the system correct.

Project Add-ons: Extra credit should be offered for integrating advanced Excel features, such as pivot tables or Visual Basic for Applications, into the home budget.

Pedagogy: This project prepares students to apply spreadsheet concepts to a practical situation, to design an attractive and easy-to-use system of spreadsheets, to organize and present related information, both graphically and textually, and to gain familiarity with a spreadsheet application (Microsoft Excel).

A.5   NETWORK-BASED INFORMATION
RETRIEVAL AND PRESENTATION

Module Placement: A course in information technology, library science, liberal arts

Task: Use network facilities on the World Wide Web to present and find information. Use a word processor to document the results.

Delivery: Home page and essay

Background: *Home Page*—The home page must consist of one page. Part of the assignment is learning to design attractive Web pages using HTML, so students should pay attention to the aesthetics of their page. The assignment also includes learning how to use a document scanner, how to convert graphics to different file formats, and how to use a text editor to produce HTML. Students can feel free to organize the information creatively; however, the page must contain the elements below:

- Some type of list, with several items;
- Several links to other sites on the Web;
- A scanned-in photo of the student;
- A graphic retrieved off the Web;
- A "mail to" form that lets visitors send a message, question, or any other information to the home page creator; and
- Table(s) to format the above content; specifically, a table should be used to format the fields and submit and reset buttons of the form.

Treasure Hunt—Students should answer the questions below using the Internet and a variety of search engines. They will also use "newsgroups" to find particular newsgroups and individual postings. Answers to the treasure hunt should be handed in as part of the networks essay. Students should provide both the answers and the sites on which the information was found.

- To whom did Jerry Garcia leave his guitars?
- What is Donald Duck's middle name?
- What environmental bill did President Clinton sign during a radio address in the fall of 1996?
- On what newsgroups should individuals . . .

    —discuss the merits of HTML tables and frames?
    —talk about yesterday's funny comic strip?
    —ask a question about algebra homework?

- On a designated class newsgroup, find the special treasure hunt posting made by a particular student (e.g., Mike) and consider his/her posting.
- Find information from another Web site that could contribute to the thread of the student's posting.

Networks Essay—Students should provide concise yet complete answers to a number of questions that focus on inter-computer communication, the Internet, and the hardware and protocols involved in networks today.

The essay should be written in Microsoft Word and should use styles to separate the answers to the background questions into logical sections.

• Describe the architecture of the Internet. As part of the answer, explain how a remote Web page is sent to your computer over the Internet, starting with you entering a Uniform Resource Locator (URL) in a browser and ending with your browser receiving the page.

• Identify and explain two obstacles to the further growth of the Internet and/or technologies relating to the Internet.

• Discuss how local area networks (LANs) are used in business and office settings. How does a LAN communicate with outside networks?

Pedagogy: This project requires students to write and design structured documents using HTML, to learn how to effectively use search engines to find information on the Internet, to become familiar with several Internet-related applications, including browsers, newsgroup readers, and graphics applications, and to learn about the Internet, protocols, and general networking concepts.

A.6 CREATING AND USING A MULTIMEDIA HYPERLINKED PRESENTATION[1]

Module Placement: A course in graphic arts, business, or non-profit administration

Task: Plan a multimedia presentation by writing a text description of the topics and points to communicate, using pictures, sound, interactive content, animation, QuickTime movies, and related materials. (It is essential that the presentation feature interactive or active content.) Select specific points from the text description where media would improve the communication potential of the presentation. Discuss with peers and select criteria to decide which medium and how many related representations are appropriate for each talking point. Design the links between the media types in order to implement the communication plan. Make links between different forms of media, and make sure that the interactive content is accessible to the intended audience. Seek criticism and guidance from experts. Try the presentation out with a pilot audience, and analyze the strengths and limitations of the presentation. Refine the presentation based on feedback from users and from experts.

---

[1] Project jointly conceived and developed with the following individuals: Michael Clancy, Eyi Chen, Tamar Posner, Lani Horn, Andrew Begel, Ricky Tang, and Phillip Bell.

Delivery: A multimedia hyperlinked presentation

Background: The creation of effective presentations involves many steps outlined above in the task. For this group project, it will be necessary to:

- Design a shared file system or e-mail attachment system to agree on tools or conversion mechanisms for the various media types and to worry about incompatibilities.
- Select tools and an environment for the multimedia presentation to ensure ease of use among the target audience. Be sure to consider platform incompatibilities, the capabilities of users, projection opportunities and venues in which the presentation might be used, and options if the first plan is unsuccessful.
- Determine the forms of help necessary in order to implement the plan on the platform selected and seek help from experts to make sure the plan is successful. Seek help as the plan gets developed to ensure it works effectively.
- Locate and select appropriate multimedia content, test it with users, and incorporate it into the presentation.

Pedagogy: Students will become familiar with considering and using multimedia to enhance a verbal presentation to an audience, to balance the multimedia and other mechanisms for presentations, to analyze what the audience learned from the presentation, and to consider modifications to meet the audience's needs more effectively.

A.7 SOCIOLOGY OF DISEASE[2]

Module Placement: A project for a biology or public health class

Task: Students are asked to imagine that they or a family member have been diagnosed with a life-threatening disease. Students should plan a course of action to find out information to answer a set of questions, and in teams of two or three, research the disease and write a paper addressing each issue. Use the search engines on the Web to gather information. Critically examine the sources of this information, and consider challenges to its validity. Coordinate the search with teammates via e-mail to avoid collecting redundant information, and review or critique each other's con-

---

[2]Project jointly conceived and developed with the following individuals: Michael Clancy, Eyi Chen, Tamar Posner, Lani Horn, Andrew Begel, Ricky Tang, and Phillip Bell.

jectures. Post papers on the class Web site, and solicit expert and peer commentary.

Delivery: Organized desription/listing of electronic resources on a variety of diseases in laymen's language

Background: The project essays should consider the following points:

• What are the alternative treatments that are effective for this disease? How do the treatments address the specific symptoms of the disease? What are the short-term and long-term consequences of the treatments?

• What social support systems are necessary to wage a successful battle against this disease? When have social support systems succeeded, and which ones? What social supports are right for this situation?

• What changes in lifestyle and diet are necessary for accommodating the symptoms and the condition of this life-threatening disease? How can these changes best be implemented and made effective?

• What other issues related to the disease are important, such as environmental factors, transmission, and discrimination? How can these be dealt with?

Pedagogy: Students will work in teams. The project will be carried out over an extended period, perhaps eight to ten weeks, with the final week devoted to student reflection on lessons learned. This project enhances researching skills and synthesis of complex information, as well as effective electronic presentation of complex data.

A.8   HOME PAGE DESIGN PROJECT[3]

Module Placement: A project for a high school computer science, English, physical science, or social science class, or an after-school activity

Task: This project requires students to design a home page for their school. The purpose of the home page is to provide information for parents researching information on the school, as well as children interested in finding out more about the school.

Delivery: A home page for a precollege school

---

[3]Project jointly conceived and developed with the following individuals: Michael Clancy, Eyi Chen, Tamar Posner, Lani Horn, Andrew Begel, Ricky Tang, and Phillip Bell.

Background: Initially, all students should work together to conceptualize the design of the site, including the main page, as well as what categories, topics, and links it should have (such as "Academics" and "Athletics"). In designing the site, students should search for Web-based tips, suggestions, and resources and also review other pages with appealing designs.

Students should then separate into groups of two to four to design a particular page on each link/topic. (Each page could include several other links.) Consulting home page exemplars should be encouraged.

The student groups should write the pages in HTML. Periodically, the entire class should meet to discuss the overall site design, share tips and examples, and discuss questions such as how to achieve consistency and the need for coherence among the different pages. These general discussions would also be a good forum in which to consider new or different technologies (e.g., different browser versions, multimedia options, user needs). Students could also test each other's pages and make suggestions. When test versions of all pages exist, students could demonstrate the site publicly and ask other students and community members to test the pages and offer comments

Pedagogy: The Web pages would be made available to the general Web community, and groups such as parents and students would be told about the appropriate address. Comments should be solicited so that new ideas could be incorporated into the existing page.

APPENDIX
B

Related Work

Judging by the scale of effort involved, many interested parties embrace the idea that knowledge of and familiarity with information technology are important to citizens. A considerable amount of work has focused on the development of educational standards to which various populations (e.g., high school students, teachers, all citizens) should be held accountable; these include standards for mathematics, science, and technology education and have been designed by various organizations. In some cases, model curricula have been developed, as well as a host of college-level courses that focus on literacy about information technology. Vocational schools and community colleges have developed programs that impart job-related technology skills, and a variety of continuing-education enterprises (both in-house and "outsourced") have been sponsored by companies for their employees.

This appendix addresses the evolving philosophy, standards, curricula, and other venues in which such educational efforts—for non-specialists—have developed an identity and/or a significant implementation in the modern world.

B.1 STANDARDS

Perhaps the earliest type of educational standard was a behavioral one, based on the notion that a student will behave in accord with a specified standard, and that the purpose of education is to induce students to behave in such a manner. Many workplace-based skill standards reflect a similar behaviorist philosophy of psychology and education.

Standards for content reflect a "knowledge-telling" philosophy of education and are the most prevalent. In this view, a student is a "blank slate" onto which the appropriate knowledge can be written. Instruction is intended to convey knowledge from teacher (or textbook) to student, and the ability to answer specific questions is the sine qua non of the educated student.

Cognitive standards reflect a more constructivist philosophy of education: the student constructs knowledge for himself or herself, perhaps guided or coached by a teacher. In doing so, the student is able to provide an appropriate context for new knowledge and is thus able to take "ownership" of that knowledge in a much more secure manner. (Much of what this report describes as intellectual capabilities is also rooted in a constructivist view of education.)

Standards are often tied to assessments rather than to instructional programs. Because the most common assessments emphasize a skill development or a "knowledge-telling" approach to instruction, instruction that putatively implements cognitive standards may in practice be quite far from constructivist instruction. Although a given set of educational standards does not necessarily imply a form of instruction, the form of instruction really does have an impact on their implementation.

The start of the modern era of educational standards can be said to date from the publication of *A Nation at Risk* in 1983,[1] which stated, "The educational foundations of our society are presently eroded by a rising tide of mediocrity that threatens our very future as a nation and a people. . . ." This report is often credited with identifying the inadequate mathematics and science preparation of U.S. students. Since its publication, efforts have followed to establish both academic and vocational (industry) standards.

In the vocational and industrial arena, *Workforce 2000* predicted in 1987 that a shortage of skilled workers would, unless checked, constrain America's economic growth.[2] In 1990, *America's Choice: High Skills or Low Wages*, explicitly called for setting academic and occupational skill standards.[3] Otherwise, the report warned, a majority of workers would continue to see their real wages decline. In 1991, the U.S. Department of

---

[1]National Commission on Excellence in Education. 1983. *A Nation at Risk: The Imperative for Educational Reform*, Department of Education, Washington, D.C., p. 65.

[2]William B. Johnston and Arnold Packer, with contributions by Matthew P. Jaffe. 1987. *Workforce 2000: Work and Workers for the Twenty-First Century*, Hudson Institute, Indianapolis, Ind., and Department of Labor, Washington, D.C., p. 117.

[3]Commission on the Skills of the American Workforce. 1990. *America's Choice: High Skill or Low Wages*, National Center on Education and the Economy, Rochester, N.Y.

Labor's Secretary's Commission on Achieving Necessary Skills (SCANS) issued *What Work Requires of Schools,* which established a language for discussing standards to ensure appropriate preparation in schools for the workplace, whether school ended with high school graduation or with completion of a Ph.D program.[4]

The National Skills Standards Board (NSSB) was created in 1994 by the National Skills Standards Act of 1994 to help voluntary industry organizations set standards for 12 industries and 4 cross-cutting occupations that will cover the entire economy. Even before NSSB was created, the U.S. Department of Labor and the Department of Education had awarded contracts to a number of groups to develop standards for such diverse areas as the retail industry, metal working, computer-aided design and computer-aided manufacture, hospitality and tourism, and even industrial launderers.

The final judgment on the NSSB effort is years away, because there are as yet no assessments for most of the jobs in most of the 16 areas that the NSSB has identified. However, some industries have begun to publish standards for selected jobs—usually at the entry level—in their spheres. The NSSB strategy involves individuals having *"core + one"* certificates. The core would be common to the entire private sector and would likely resemble the workplace know-how defined by the SCANS commission.

In the academic arena, the National Council of Teachers of Mathematics (NCTM) produced the first set of national mathematics content standards for K-12 education, *Curriculum and Evaluation Standards for School Mathematics,* released in 1989.[5] (NCTM also produced *Professional Standards for Teaching Mathematics* (1991)[6] and *Assessment Standards for School Mathematics* (1995).[7]) Also in 1989, the American Association for the Advancement of Science, through its Project 2061 program, published *Science for All Americans,*[8] which defined scientific literacy for all high school graduates. In 1993, Project 2061 issued a content-oriented document,

---

[4]Commission on Standards for School Mathematics. 1989. *What Work Requires of Schools: A SCANS Report for America 2000,* Department of Labor, Washington, D.C.

[5]Commission on Standards for School Mathematics. 1989. *Curriculum and Evaluation Standards for School Mathematics,* National Council of Teachers of Mathematics, Reston, Va.

[6]Commission on Standards for School Mathematics. 1991. *Professional Standards for Teaching Mathematics,* National Council of Teachers of Mathematics, Reston, Va.

[7]Commission on Standards for School Mathematics. 1991. *Assessment Standards for School Mathematics,* National Council of Teachers of Mathematics, Reston, Va.

[8]American Association for the Advancement of Science. 1989. *Science for All Americans: A Project 2061 Report on Literacy Goals in Science, Mathematics, and Technology,* American Association for the Advancement of Science, Washington, D.C.

Benchmarks for Science Literacy.[9]   The National Research Council deliberated on appropriate science content for precollege education and issued *National Science Education Standards* in 1996.[10] Continuing the new era of reform, the International Technology Education Association will publish technology standards for K-12 education in 1999.

Furthermore, states have been establishing their own academic standards for high school graduation, although there is still great confusion over what makes for an adequate standard. The American Federation of Teachers, the Council for Basic Education, and the Fordham Foundation have attempted to rate state efforts, although an *Education Week* analysis found large disparities in the letter grades assigned by these organizations.[11] For example, more than half the states received marks in mathematics that varied by at least two letter grades across the three organizations' reports. In English/language arts, such variability was found in 19 states. Finally, a quite recent analysis found that there is a long way to go before "standards-based reform" becomes a reality in the nation's schools.[12]

In general, the academic standards described above differ from the results of past efforts at education reform in two important ways. First, they emphasize the goals of literacy and broad inclusion, rather than concentrating on an intellectually elite subpopulation. Second, they identify an important role for whole communities (rather than just teachers); everyone plays some part in assisting educators to meet the standards. For example, in *National Science Education Standards*, business and industry are asked to collaborate with school personnel to initiate interesting, high-quality programs that support the standards.[13] Legislators and public officials are asked to strive for policies and funding priorities that support the goals of the standards.

As envisioned by their authoring bodies, the standards present content—not curriculum—to facilitate coordination, consistency, and coherence of mathematics, science, and technology education in the United States. They are designed to encourage a consistent set of educational outcomes that develop students' critical thinking skills, scientific reason-

---

[9]American Association for the Advancement of Science. 1993. *Benchmarks for Science Literacy*, Oxford University Press, New York.

[10]National Research Council. 1996. *National Science Education Standards*, National Academy Press, Washington, D.C.

[11]Lynn Olson. 1998. *Education Week*, April 15.

[12]Mark Tucker and Judy Codding. 1998. *Standards for Our Schools*, Jossey-Bass Publishers, San Francisco, Calif.

[13]National Research Council. 1996. *National Science Education Standards*, National Academy Press, Washington D.C., p. 245.

ing, creative problem solving, and judicious analysis—qualities identified by various constituencies as critical to the nation's ability to meet the scientific and technological demands of the 21st century and remain competitive in an increasingly global economy.

Although the distinction does provide a good point of departure for understanding standards, the line between academic and vocational/ industrial standards is somewhat blurred. For example, the SCANS approach was supported by the Department of Labor, but leaned in the direction of academic standards.

Other government agencies have not been silent, and other standards have been developed. The National Institute for Literacy has an ongoing project, Equip for the Future (EFF), which has recently published draft literacy content standards for three realms: work, citizenship, and parenting. This work follows on earlier efforts such as the Educational Testing Services' International Adult Literacy Survey, which was based on a three-part structure of prose, document, and quantitative literacy. The EFF framework describes for each of three roles (work, citizenship, and parenting) four purposes: access to information, a voice in individuals' own lives, ability to take action, and a bridge to the future (learning to learn). For all of these the EFF defined 12 common activities (such as management of resources). It then defined 17 generative skills (such as interpersonal skills) and knowledge domains (such as systems) that support the common activities. In many ways, the EFF framework can be seen as an elaboration on the SCANS approach.

A wide range of standards at the industry, federal, and the state level have begun to evolve and help define the scope and meaning of information technology literacy and related concepts. The subsections below identify some of the most salient standards as they relate to the committee's idea of fluency with information technology (FITness).

B.1.1   National Council of Teachers of Mathematics Standards

In its 1989 report, *Curriculum and Evaluation Standards for School Mathematics*, the National Council of Teachers of Mathematics (NCTM) defined mathematical literacy as the combination of five interrelated goals for students:[14]

1. Learn to value mathematics,
2. Become confident in their ability to do mathematics,

---

[14]Commission on Standards for School Mathematics. 1989. *Curriculum and Evaluation Standards for School Mathematics*, National Council of Teachers of Mathematics, Reston, Va., p. 5.

3. Become mathematical problem solvers,
4. Learn to communicate mathematically, and
5. Learn to reason mathematically.

The NCTM standards are intended to provide a coherent framework for ensuring "that all students have an opportunity to become mathematically literate, are capable of extending their learning, [and] have an equal opportunity to learn."[15] Importantly, the rationale for these standards is couched in terms of the mathematical literacy needed to function in an information and technological society. For example, the report states that "technology has dramatically changed the nature of the physical, life, and social sciences; business; industry; and government . . . . Information is the new capital and the new material, and communication is the new means of production. . . . The impact of this technological shift has become an economic reality. Today, the pace of economic change is being accelerated by continued innovation in communications and computer technology."[16]

Finally, the NCTM standards are envisioned as a living document; a working group is now revising the initial set of standards (Box B.1 gives an example from the current NCTM curriculum), and an updated version is expected in the year 2000.

B.1.2   Standards for Science Education

The standards set forth in the National Research Council's *National Science Education Standards* were developed "to provide criteria to judge progress toward a national vision of learning and teaching science in a system that promotes excellence. . . ."[17] Approximately four years of deliberations and the combined work of thousands of educators, scientists, science educators, and other experts nationwide produced a comprehensive vision of effective science education. The associated standards

---

[15]Commission on Standards for School Mathematics. 1989. *Curriculum and Evaluation Standards for School Mathematics*, National Council of Teachers of Mathematics, Reston, Va., p. 5.
[16]Commission on Standards for School Mathematics. 1989. *Curriculum and Evaluation Standards for School Mathematics*, National Council of Teachers of Mathematics, Reston, Va., p. 3.
[17]National Research Council. 1996. *National Science Education Standards,* National Academy Press, Washington D.C., p. 12.

Box B.1
Sample NCTM Curriculum Standard—Functions

In grades 9-12, the mathematics curriculum should include the continued study of functions so that all students can—

• model real-world phenomena with a variety of functions;
• represent and analyze relationships using tables, verbal rules, equations, and graphs;
• translate among tabular, symbolic, and graphical representations of functions;
• recognize that a variety of problem situations can be modeled by the same type of function;
• analyze the effects of parameter changes on the graphs of functions;

and so that, in addition, college-intending students can—

• understand operations on, and the general properties and behavior of, classes of functions. . . .

. . . The function concept also is important because it is a mathematical representation of many input-output situations found in the real world, including those that recently have arisen as a result of technological advances. . . .

Since functional relationships are encountered so frequently, the study of functions should begin with a sampling of those that exist in the students' world. Students should have the opportunity to appreciate the pervasiveness of functions through activities such as describing real-world relationships that can be depicted by graphs, reading and interpreting graphs, and sketching graphs of data in which the value of one variable depends on the value of another.

SOURCE: Excerpted from Commission on Standards for School Mathematics. 1989. *Curriculum and Evaluation Standards for School Mathematics,* National Council of Teachers of Mathematics, Reston, Va., pp. 154-155.

outline the content of what students need to know, understand, and be able to do to be scientifically literate at all grade levels. In addition, they address pedagogy, professional development, assessment, individual school programs, and public policy at various levels. The standards are intended to guide local educational administrators and educators in formulating curricula, staff development activities, and assessment programs.

National Science Education Standards reflects the conviction that science understanding and ability will "enhance the capability of all students to hold meaningful and productive jobs in the future," in a business community that needs workers who can "learn, reason, think creatively, make decisions, and solve problems."[18]

An example of the NRC's science education content standards is provided in Box B.2.

B.1.3   Technology for All Americans Project

Historically, the United States has neglected technology education in its academic repertoire, relegating the understanding of technology—the study of the human-made world—to vocational education.[19]   In European countries such as Germany, trade schools have long prepared children of workers for entry into the workforce.[20]   Now, standards for technology education are being created by the International Technology Education Association (ITEA), and they will serve as the basis for promoting technological literacy in grades K-12.   A document produced in the first phase of the project, *Technology for All Americans: A Rationale and Structure for the Study of Technology,* defines the need for standards for technology education and shows how technology can be studied.[21]   This phase has also sought to build consensus on issues concerning technology education.

Phase II of the project will develop standards for technology education at all grade levels, K-12.   The standards will focus on what students need to know and be able to do in order to be technologically literate. The standards document will identify appropriate content for technology education in a comprehensive but flexible format that local administrators and educators can adapt to fit their particular academic curriculum.

The goal of technology standards is to foster technology-literate students.   ITEA defines technology literacy as ". . . knowing how to use, manage, and understand technology."[22]   One purpose of these standards

---

[18]National Research Council. 1996. *National Science Education Standards,* National Academy Press, Washington D.C., p. 12.

[19]International Technology Education Association. 1996. *Technology for All Americans: A Rationale and Structure for the Study of Technology,* International Technology Education Association, Reston, Va.

[20]Thomas Alexander. 1918. *The Prussian Elementary Schools,* Macmillan, New York.

[21]*Technology for All Americans: A Rationale and Structure for the Study of Technology,* 1996.

[22]*Technology for All Americans: A Rationale and Structure for the Study of Technology,* 1996, Chapter 2, p. 9.

Box B.2
Sample Science Education Standard

CONTENT STANDARD B [Physical Science]: As a result of their activities in grades 9-12, all students should develop an understanding of

- Structure of atoms
- Structure and properties of matter
- Chemical reactions
- Motions and forces
- Conservation of energy and increase in disorder
- Interactions of energy and matter

DEVELOPING STUDENT UNDERSTANDING

High-school students develop the ability to relate the macroscopic properties of substances that they study in grades K-8 to the microscopic structure of substances. This development in understanding requires students to move among three domains of thought—the macroscopic world of observable phenomena, the microscopic world of molecules, atoms, and subatomic particles, and the symbolic and mathematical world of chemical formulas, equations, and symbols. . . .

On the basis of their experiences with energy transfers in the middle grades, high-school students can investigate energy transfers quantitatively by measuring variables such as temperature change and kinetic energy. Laboratory investigations and descriptions of other experiments can help students understand the evidence that leads to the conclusion that energy is conserved. Although the operational distinction between temperature and heat can be fairly well understood after careful instruction, research with high-school students indicates that the idea that heat is the energy of

is to strengthen educators' recognition of technology as a dynamic, transforming force that schools must prepare students and citizens to manage effectively, given its increasingly central role in U.S. economic, social, and political systems. In equipping students with technology literacy, a standards-based curriculum prepares graduates to become "vested members of our technologically based society, contributing members of our workforce, and cognizant members of our democracy."[23]

The ITEA's *Technology for All Americans* standards are expected to be released in 2000.

---

[23]*Technology for All Americans: A Rationale and Structure for the Study of Technology*, 1996, Chapter 1, p. 3.

random motion and vibrating molecules is difficult for students to understand.

GUIDE TO THE CONTENT STANDARD

Fundamental concepts and principles that underlie this standard include . . . Conservation of Energy and the Increase in Disorder.

- The total energy of the universe is constant. Energy can be transferred by collisions in chemical and nuclear reactions, by light waves and other radiation, and in many other ways. However, it can never be destroyed. As these transfers occur, the matter involved becomes steadily less ordered.
- All energy can be considered to be either kinetic energy, which is the energy of motion; potential energy, which depends on relative position; or energy contained by a field, such as electromagnetic waves.
- Heat consists of random motion and the vibrations of atoms, molecules, and ions. The higher the temperature, the greater the atomic or molecular motion.
- Everything tends to become less organized and less orderly over time. Thus, in all energy transfers, the overall effect is that the energy is spread out uniformly. Examples are the transfer of energy from hotter to cooler objects by conduction, radiation, or convection and the warming of our surroundings when we burn fuels.

SOURCE: Excerpted from National Research Council. 1996. "Content Standards: 9-12," in *National Science Education Standards*, National Academy Press, Washington, D.C., pp. 176-178.

B.1.4   National Educational Technology Standards Project

The International Society for Technology in Education (ISTE) has produced a set of guidelines for technology skills in pre-K through 12th grade education, the *National Educational Technology Standards for Students (NETS)*.[24]   The primary goal of the NETS project has been "to develop national standards for the educational uses of technology. . . to guide educational leaders in recognizing and addressing the essential conditions

---

[24]International Society for Technology in Education. 1988. *National Educational Technology Standards for Students*, International Society for Technology in Education, Eugene, Ore. Available online at <http:// cnets.iste.org/>.

for effective use of technology to support PreK-12 education." The premise for these guidelines is the belief that the U.S. educational system must begin the complex task of integrating technology within a sound educational system to prepare students for the opportunities and rigors of the technologically rich 21st century.

The technology foundation standards for students are divided into six broad categories:

1. Basic operations and concepts (students demonstrate a sound understanding of the nature and operation of technology systems and are proficient in the use of technology).

2. Social, ethical, and human issues (students understand the ethical, cultural, and societal issues related to technology; practice responsible use of technology systems, information, and software; and develop positive attitudes toward technology uses that support lifelong learning, collaboration, personal pursuits, and productivity).

3. Technology productivity tools (students use technology tools to enhance learning, increase productivity, promote creativity, and use productivity tools to collaborate in constructing technology-enhanced models, preparing publications, and producing other creative works).

4. Technology communications tools (students use telecommunications to collaborate, publish, interact with peers, experts, and other audiences, and use a variety of media and formats to communicate information and ideas effectively to multiple audiences).

5. Technology research tools (students use technology to locate, evaluate, and collect information from a variety of sources; use technology tools to process data and report results; and evaluate and select new information resources and technological innovations based on their appropriateness to specific tasks).

6. Technology problem-solving and decision-making tools (students use technology resources for solving problems and making informed decisions, and employ technology in the development of strategies for solving problems in the real world).

To assist teachers, ISTE has also created a general set of profiles that describe technology literate students at key developmental points in their pre-college education. These profiles provide performance indicators describing the technology competence students should exhibit upon completion of the various grade ranges (see Box B.3, for example).

Box B.3
Sample Profile for Technology Literate Students (Grades 9-12)

Students will:

1. Identify capabilities and limitations of contemporary and emerging technology resources and assess the potential of these systems and services to address personal, lifelong learning, and workplace needs. (2)[1]

2. Make informed choices among technology systems, resources, and services. (1,2)

3. Analyze advantages and disadvantages of widespread use of and reliance on technology in the workplace and in society as a whole. (2)

4. Demonstrate and advocate for legal and ethical behaviors among peers, family, and community regarding the use of technology and information. (2)

5. Use technology tools and resources for managing and communicating personal/professional information (e.g., finances, schedules, addresses, purchases, correspondence). (3, 4)

6. Evaluate technology-based options, including distance and distributed education, for lifelong learning. (5)

7. Routinely and efficiently use online information resources to meet needs for collaboration, research, publications, communications, and productivity. (4, 5, 6)

8. Select and apply technology tools for research, information analysis, problem-solving, and decision-making in content learning. (4, 5)

9. Investigate and apply expert systems, intelligent agents, and simulations in real-world situations. (3, 5, 6)

10. Collaborate with peers, experts, and others to contribute to a content-related knowledge base by using technology to compile, synthesize, produce, and disseminate information, models, and other creative works. (4, 5, 6)

SOURCE: This material is taken from the "Profiles for Students" section of a Web page provided by the International Society for Technology in Education. Available online at <http://cnets.iste.org/>.

[1] Numbers in parentheses following each performance indicator refer to the standards category to which the performance is linked.

B.1.5   The Secretary's Commission on Achieving Necessary Skills

In 1992, the Department of Labor's Secretary's Commission on Achieving Necessary Skills (SCANS) released *Learning a Living: A Blueprint for High Performance*,[25] which identified the skills needed by Americans to join the growing high-skill workforce. As described in the report, the commission's fundamental purpose was "to encourage a high-performance economy characterized by high-skill, high-wage employment" (p. xiii).

The commission addressed its messages to three stakeholders. Schools were asked to expand their mission to include the diverse roles students will eventually play in their communities and workplaces. Teachers were encouraged to adopt an interdisciplinary and global teaching approach, including making connections to instill a broader perspective. Employers were urged to improve the organization of work and the development of human resources, with greater consideration for the community and the country as well as the company.

The conclusions and recommendations—aimed at "reinventing school," "fostering work-based learning," "reorganizing the workplace," and "restructuring assessment"—are grounded in five workplace competencies and three foundational skills that the commission proposed as a national blueprint by which to judge competence in necessary high-technology skills. The competencies, skills, and personal qualities were identified as fundamental requirements for building a workforce prepared to lead advancements and participate effectively in the information age. These goals were advocated for all students.

Box B.4 describes how the SCANS competencies and FITness capabilities relate to each other.

B.1.6   State Standards for Technology Literacy

Some states, such as New York and Maine, have begun to develop standards for K-12 technology education. The Maine standards tend to treat technology literacy as a supporting skill within the sciences, as suggested by the subject area heading "science and technology," rather than as a separate subject area.[26]

---

[25]Secretary's Commission on Achieving Necessary Skills. 1992. *Learning a Living: A Blueprint for High Performance*, Department of Labor, Washington, D.C.

[26]Maine Department of Education. 1996. "State of Maine Learning Results," Draft, Maine Department of Education, Augusta, Maine, December. Available online at <HtmlResAnchor http://www.state.me.us/education/lres.htm>.

The New York State standards (revised in March 1996) reflect a more constructivist view, focusing on technology competency so that students will be able to apply technological knowledge and skills to design, construct, use, and evaluate products and systems to satisfy human and environmental needs.[27] Although they are more elaborate than the Maine standards, the New York standards also fit within a collection of standards that address scientific and technological literacy. Each standard identifies content for appropriate learning and requirements at the elementary, intermediate, and high school levels.

New York State's technology standards encompass seven different areas of investigation and education as described below:

- *Engineering design:* Modeling and optimization are used in an iterative process to develop technological solutions to problems within given constraints.
- *Tools, resources, and technological processes:* Technological tools, materials, and other resources should be selected on the basis of safety, cost, availability, appropriateness, and environmental impact; technological processes change energy, information, and material resources into more useful forms.
- *Computers:* As tools for design, modeling, information processing, communication, and system control, computers have greatly increased human productivity and knowledge.
- *Technological systems:* Systems are designed to achieve specific results and produce outputs, such as products, structures, services, energy, or other systems.
- *History and evolution of technology:* Technology has been the driving force in the evolution of society from an agricultural to an industrial to an information base.
- *Impact of technology:* Technology can have positive and negative impacts on individuals, society, and the environment, and humans have the capability and responsibility to constrain or promote technological development.
- *Management of technology:* Project management is essential to ensuring that technological endeavors are profitable and that products and systems are of high quality and built safely, on schedule, and within budget.

The standards for students range from using materials in the elemen-

---

[27]New York State Department of Education. 1996. *Learning Standards for Mathematics, Science, and Technology*, revised edition, Albany, New York.

Box B.4
The SCANS Framework and FITness

A particularly important viewpoint is presented in the SCANS report produced in 1992 by the Secretary of Labor's Commission on Achieving Necessary Skills to promote the development of a skilled workforce.[1] In addition to being the driver for a number of efforts (ranging from programs for literacy to standards for the retail industry and the information technology industry), the SCANS report described competencies that provided an important point of departure for the approach to FITness described in Chapter 2 of this report. The SCANS workplace competencies include the following:

1. *Planning and resource allocation* (budgets, schedules, space, and staff);
2. *Information* (acquire, evaluate, interpret, organize, communicate);
3. *Interpersonal skills* (work in teams, negotiate, teach, lead, serve customers, work with diversity);
4. *Technology* (select, use, and troubleshoot);
5. *Systems* (understand, monitor, and design).

The intellectual framework laid out in this report and the SCANS report have much in common. In particular, the SCANS competencies are expressed in the context of sustained collaborative project activity, using technology. The correspondence between the FITness capabilities and the SCANS competencies is shown in Table B.1 below.

---

[1]Secretary's Commission on Achieving Necessary Skills. 1992. *Learning a Living: A Blueprint for High Performance*, Department of Labor, Washington, D.C.

---

tary grades to understanding and considering the societal impacts of the adopted technologies as a commencement requirement. Box B.5 provides some examples of standards that must be met upon graduation from high school.

B.1.7   Information Technology Skill Standards[28]

The National Science Foundation (NSF) is funding a number of efforts to develop standards for information technology skills. Bellevue

---

[28]This description is adapted from a Web page on information technology skill standards provided by the Northwest Center for Emerging Technologies at Bellevue Community College in Bellevue, Washington. The page can be found at <HtmlResAnchor http://nwcet.bcc.ctc.edu/skills/intro/intro.htm>.

TABLE B.1   A Comparison of FITness Capabilities and SCANS Workplace Competencies

FITness Capabilities	SCANS Competencies
1. Engage in sustained reasoning	Pedagogical strategy
2. Manage complexity	Systems (Monitor)
3. Manage problems in faulty solutions	Systems (Design)
4. Test a solution	Systems (Design)
8. Expect the unexpected	Systems (Understand, monitor)
9. Anticipate changing technologies	Systems (Understand, monitor)
10. Think about information technology abstractly	Systems (Understand)
6. Collaborate	Interpersonal Skills
5. Organize and navigate information structures	Information (Organize, evaluate)
7. Communicate to other audiences	Information (Communicate)

The SCANS competencies are as "deep" and intellectually demanding as the FITness capabilities. For example, the Information competency includes the ability to write coherent and persuasive prose as well as effectively use a word processor. Moreover, the SCANS competencies have been found to apply to domains other than employment. An understanding of economics and the federal budget is as important to the average citizen as understanding copyright and encryption.

Community College in Bellevue, Washington, is the host for the Northwest Center for Emerging Technologies (NWCET). In addition to its five-year NSF funding, the center has received support from Boeing and from Microsoft. To support the needs of industry, NWCET has defined standards for eight information technology positions (career clusters): database administration associate, information systems operator/analyst, interactive digital media specialist, network specialist, programmer/analyst, software engineer, technical support representative, and technical writer. (Box B.6 provides further discussion and details.) Although it began at a different starting point, NWCET has come to many of the same conclusions as this and the SCANS report.

Determined and validated through an extensive survey process, these standards were developed to establish agreed-upon, industry-identified

Box B.5
Sample Criteria from New York State Technology Standards:
High School Level

To demonstrate technology competency in the seven areas described in the main text, students should be able to do the following in each area (only selected items are provided):

• *Engineering design:* Initiate an investigation, identify needs and opportunities for technological invention and innovation, generate creative solution ideas, break ideas into the significant functional elements, and explore possible refinements.

• *Tools, resources and technological processes:* Explain trade-offs, and describe and model methods to control processes and monitor system outputs.

• *Computer technology:* Understand basic computer architecture and describe the function of computer subsystems and peripheral devices; select a computer system that meets personal needs; attach a modem to a computer system and telephone line, set up and use communications software, connect to various online networks, including the Internet, and access needed information using e-mail, telnet, gopher, ftp, and Web searches.

• *Technological systems:* Explain why making trade-offs among characteristics, such as safety, function, cost, ease of operation, quality of post-purchase support, and environmental impact, is necessary when selecting systems for specific purposes; explain how complex technological systems involve the confluence of numerous other systems.

• *History and evolution of technology:* Explain how technological inventions have caused global growth and interdependence, stimulated economic competitiveness, created new jobs, and made other jobs obsolete.

• *Impacts of technology:* Explain that although technological effects are complex and difficult to predict accurately, humans can control the development and implementation of technology; explain how computers and automation have changed the nature of work.

• *Management of technology:* Use computer-based scheduling and project tracking tools; discuss the role of technology in successful U.S. businesses; help to manage a group to gain understanding of the management of dynamics.

SOURCE: Adapted from New York State Department of Education. 1996. *Learning Standards for Mathematics, Science, and Technology,* revised edition, Albany, New York, pp. 50-53.

Box B.6
An Example of the NWCET Standards

The technology standards of the Northwest Center for Emerging Technologies (NWCET) are tied to specific types of jobs. For example, a programmer analyst (also known as a systems analyst, an applications analyst, an applications engineer, an operating systems programmer/analyst, an operating systems engineer, or a test engineer) is said to analyze, design, develop, test, implement, and maintain computer applications systems to meet functional objectives of a business. His or her job functions include analysis, design, development, testing, implementation, project management, and task management.

To establish a context, the standards provide a thumbnail job description:

As a Programmer or Analyst, you design and update the software that runs the computer. . . . Often, you'll participate in design meetings where you help determine the best way to approach a problem or implement a desired feature for the new version of the software. Because of the complexity of the software and because parts of the software interconnect, this can take quite some time, depending on the magnitude of the change. You most likely will also be responsible for writing the specifications and keeping the specifications current for your part of the software.

You'll code the changes, and then test and debug the software, which may take a year or more of intense and focused work, including evenings and weekends. The challenge, of course, is to keep the software as lean as possible, while making it robust, powerful, and expandable. In most cases, the Programmer, Analyst, or Engineer must also ensure backwards compatibility with application software written for previous versions of the software. Periodically, the software team compiles the code. This software build is tested, and you correct any problems which fall into your area of the code.

The core of the standards is a description of the primary tasks and functions involved in this scenario. These tasks and functions are selected from longer "master" lists of tasks and functions on the basis of their applicability to the scenario provided. For example, the scenario described above calls for the following:

• *Analysis* (gather data to identify customer requirements; interpret and evaluate requirements; define scope of work to meet customer requirements; develop high-level systems and functional specifications; develop alternatives),

• *Design* (develop detailed design specifications; develop entity relationships; prepare and conduct design review), and

• *Project management* (evaluate project requirements; report on project status).

SOURCE: Adapted from material found online at <http://nwcet.bcc.ctc.edu/skills/example/paf.htm>.

knowledge, skills, and abilities required to succeed in the workplace, thus providing benchmarks of skill and performance attainment that are behavioral and measurable. Without such information, employers do not know whom to hire or how to evaluate employees, employees and new entrants to the workforce do not know what is expected of them, and educators do not know how to prepare students for the challenges of the workplace. Industry-identified skill standards also serve as a vehicle for companies to communicate their expectations for worker performance. Skill standards provide a common framework for communication of workplace expectations between business, education, workers, students, and government.

B.2 PHILOSOPHY

One influential author who has explored the potential of information technology as a tool for reconceptualizing the educational process is Seymour Papert.[29] As noted in Chapter 1, Papert believes that a deep understanding of programming can result in many significant educational benefits in many domains of discourse, including those unrelated to computers and information technology per se. However, he also expresses concern about the education community's conventional response to the call for increased integration of computer technology into the school by creating computer labs and a formal learning sequence comparable to that of other elective business courses. While "assimilating" computers into the traditional system is a natural first step, Papert asserts that the computer cannot be a transforming tool within the rigid constraints of traditional school structure. Instead, he believes that students can experience the genuine power of computers to transform their educational understanding, and ultimately develop new ways of thinking, only through a more fluid, freer environment of exploration. For this to occur, computers must be integrated throughout the curriculum, including leaving room to revise and reform the curriculum. This objective must be pursued by teachers who are comfortable with computers and with a creative and unrestricted structure, and who are supported by a like-minded educational community.

A complementary view regarding information technology literacy is offered in the report *Digital Literacy: Survival Skills for the Information Age* (BiT3M partners, under the auspices of SRI Consulting), which was commissioned to address how to create a digitally literate workforce. The

---

[29]Seymour A. Papert. 1999. *Mindstorms: Children, Computers, and Powerful Ideas*, Second Edition, Basic Books, New York.

report defines digital literacy as "the ability to communicate successfully using digitally encoded information in any medium or format" (p. 1), and it states that to survive and prosper in the information age, people must learn new skills and knowledge to become digitally literate. Those who do will be empowered to use the digital medium effectively; those who do not will be increasingly excluded.

The report describes literacy as cumulative, without a definitive set of symbols and images to master. Rather, literacy is a competency—an ability to produce a useful result—requiring a combination of knowledge, skills, and attitude. The three broad categories defined to cover users' differing needs for digital literacy are technical, informational, and cultural. Developing digital literacy requires a combination of formal instruction, self-instruction, trial and error, peer discussion, and a computer's online help facility. The report concludes that, although technology is destined to become more powerful and applications easier to use, the informational and cultural qualities of digital literacy are becoming increasingly important but also more difficult to master. These qualities depend on having the skills and knowledge "to ensure that [technology reflects] our values and assumptions or, at least, that we understand [technology]" (p. 11).

B.3   MODEL CURRICULA AND COURSES

B.3.1   ACM Model High School Computer Science Curriculum

The ACM (originally the Association for Computing Machinery) produced recommendations for college-level computer science curricula in 1968, 1978, and 1991. In 1989, the Pre-College Committee of the Education Board of the ACM addressed the need for a high school computer science curriculum standard. Aimed at 10th grade, the ACM "Model High School Computer Science Curriculum" was originally published in 1993.[30] It proposed that computer science education should be required for all high school students, similar to the curriculum requirements for the natural sciences: "The study of computer science is composed of basic universal concepts that transcend the technology and that comprise an essential part of a high school education. It is these concepts that enable the student to understand and participate effectively in our modern world." The recommended topics and areas listed below are based on this premise.

---

[30]Task Force of the Pre-College Committee of the Education Board of the ACM. 1993. "Model High School Computer Science Curriculum," *Communications of the ACM*, 36(5): 87-90.

Informed by the ACM computing curriculum for colleges and universities, the ACM model curriculum for high school computer science identifies the following core topics:

- Algorithms;
- Programming languages;
- Operating systems and user support;
- Computer architecture;
- Social, ethical, and professional context; and
- Computer applications.

Core content is specified in all topics except computer applications, for which it is recommended that applications in the following areas be included:

- Computer aided design/computer aided manufacturing;
- Computer speech, music synthesis, and art;
- Database systems;
- Electronic mail and bulletin boards;
- Multimedia and presentation graphics;
- Scientific analysis (e.g., Mathematica, Mathlab), spreadsheets, and data analysis;
- Word processing and desktop publishing.

Other "additional topics" were also recommended to illustrate the current state of the art in the computer science discipline itself. Examples include the following:

- Artificial intelligence, e.g., games, expert systems, robotics, knowledge representations;
- Computational science, e.g., scientific visualization, modeling;
- Graphics, e.g., image generation, two- and three-dimensional animation;
- Simulation and virtual reality;
- Software engineering, e.g., system development, software development cycle, modeling, and diagramming.

Secondary schools have not embraced computer science as an essential discipline for all students, and so the ACM model high school curriculum has not been widely implemented. Instead, students with a special gift or interest in computer science can, in some high schools, take an Advanced Placement course in computer science. This type of curriculum, however, is far more specialized (focused on programming) than that which would meet the FITness needs of high school students.

B.3.2   College-level Courses

For many years, college computer science programs have offered courses for non-majors. These courses have evolved rapidly as technology has evolved. Some years ago, they concentrated on teaching students basic skills with word processing, spreadsheets, and presentation graphics. Today, many of these courses provide experience with Web page design and use of the Internet for communication. Overall, however, these courses have had a rather limited vision, one of providing basic technological skills to students who might use them in their own major field of study.

More recently, some colleges and universities have added a specific computer literacy requirement for graduation. This requirement is defined in various ways, depending on the kinds and amount of faculty resources that can be dedicated to these courses. For example, students at Marist College fulfill its computer literacy requirement by completing any one of a variety of 1-credit courses taught by faculty in different disciplines.[31] Other institutions of higher education, like Wake Forest University, are engaged in vigorous faculty development projects that will help individual faculty members learn to integrate the use of technology into existing courses across the curriculum.[32] Still others, like Bowdoin College, take a more laissez-faire approach, expecting that their faculty and students will, by one means or another, become computer literate without any special efforts as they progress through their course work.

Most colleges and universities now provide a full range of computing and networking resources,[33] expecting that their students will use technology effectively in their various courses of study. Overall, many believe[34] that we have entered the era of ubiquitous computing on college campuses, an era in which computers are commonplace and inexpensive, and are effectively deployed to serve the needs of all students and faculty.

The content of specific computer literacy courses for non-computer science majors varies widely among colleges. Many of these courses are

---

[31]See <http://vm.marist.edu:80/~courinfo/descriptions/csis.html>.

[32]See, for example, < http://www.wfu.edu/CELI>.

[33]See <http://www.bowdoin.edu/cwis/admissions/resources/electronic.html>, for example.

[34]Mark Weiser. 1998. "The Future of Ubiquitous Computing on Campus," *Communications of the ACM*, 41(January):41-42.

limited to teaching a collection of skills with modern software packages, and thus do not embrace the idea of FITness as it is described in the main body of this report. However, there are some exceptions. At Duke University, the computer literacy course focuses on the theme "what computers can do and what they can't do, now and in the future."[35] It assumes no prior computing experience, and in a single semester introduces students to the fundamentals of programming, hardware and software, and the limits of computation. At Brown University, the computer literacy course "Concepts and Challenges of Computer Science" introduces students to programming and other problem-solving tools, as well as a wide range of topics that relate computing to daily life.[36] Sample assignments in this course include home budgets, client database management, and writing a Java script to play the game tic-tac-toe. At both Duke and Brown, the computer literacy courses are hands-on laboratory-based courses with a high level of interaction among students and instructors.

Vocational and technical colleges also offer a wide range of courses that contribute to information technology literacy. For instance, the University of Maine at Augusta offers a two-year degree program in computer and information systems. The core curriculum covers various areas of technology, including computer systems, networking, databases, administration of computing facilities, applications programming, and working with the World Wide Web. It emphasizes hands-on learning and practical applications of information systems.[37]

B.4   OTHER APPROACHES TO
INFORMATION TECHNOLOGY LITERACY

Skills with and knowledge about information technology may also be gained through various informal channels. For instance, dozens of teenagers and community leaders have benefited from the U.S. West Foundation's New Technology Academy, which uses children as teachers of computer technology. This program is hoping to spread the word that even in the poorest communities, kids with their uninhibited curiosity and wealth of time to "fiddle and explore" may very well be the nation's most natural teachers and maintainers of technology. Programs that use young computer "whizzes" as "computer-maintenance technicians,

---

[35]Alan W. Biermann. 1994. "Computer Science for the Many," *Computer*, 27(February):62-73.

[36]See, for example, <http://www.cs.brown.edu/courses/cs002>.

[37]See <http://www.uma.maine.edu/academics/uacadcisbrochure.html>.

troubleshooters and one-on-one tutors for fellow students, teachers and even school principals" are popping up across the nation.[38]

B.4.1 ACM Code of Ethics

The ACM Code of Ethics and Professional Conduct is designed as a guide for computer professionals.[39] The code is very pragmatic and necessarily has an information technology literacy component. Moreover, it reflects the expectation that ACM members not only remain technically competent themselves but also contribute to the technical education of others. Although the code has little information about specific technological competencies, it does require that members conduct their lives in a way that respects the copyright, privacy, and other ethical aspects of technology and digital information that they encounter in their work.

B.4.2 On- and Off-the-Job Training

The skills for learning about e-mail, voice mail, "netiquette," and the impact of electronic communication on an organization are often taught in-house. The advantage is that curricula can be customized to the particular needs of the organization. For example, Kinko's information technology training needs are satisfied by extensive on-the-job training and a 2-hour course that teaches the basics of files, disk storage, hierarchies, directories, removable media, and networks, in a Windows or Macintosh environment.

A number of private companies, such as CompUSA (http://www.compusa.com) and New Horizons (http://www.newhorizons.com), offer information technology training courses for the employees of large organizations and individuals. For example, CompUSA "offers computer training for the corporate client as well as the general public. It specializes in the programs that people use at home and in the office. Classes are generally offered six days a week and twice a week during the evenings. There are over 150 CompUSA Training Centers located nationwide with several new Training SuperCenter Plus sites opening in greater metropolitan areas. The new centers specialize in Novell software, project management software, Visual Basic, Lotus Notes, and Microsoft Access."

---

[38]Elizabeth Heilman Brook. 1998. "Whiz Kids Are Given a Chance to Teach Their Stuff," *New York Times*, April 23. Available online at <HtmlResAnchor http://www.nytimes.com/library/tech/98/04/circuits/articles/23kids.html>.

[39]For more information, see <http://www.acm.org/constitution/code.html>.

APPENDIX
C

Individuals Who Briefed the Committee

August 19-20, 1997

John C. Cherniavsky, Office of Cross-Disciplinary Activities, CISE Directorate, National Science Foundation

Peter J. Denning, Computer Science Department, George Mason University

Nancy Devino, Committee on Undergraduate Science Education, National Research Council

Barry W. Johnson, Department of Electrical Engineering, University of Virginia

Pam B. Newberry, Technology for All Americans Project

Greg Pearson, National Academy of Engineering

Harold Pratt, Division on K-12 Policy and Practice, National Research Council

William A. Wulf, National Academy of Engineering

April 3-4, 1998

Andrea diSessa, Graduate School of Education, University of California, Berkeley

Mark Guzdial, Graphics Visualization and Usability Center, College of Computing, Georgia Institute of Technology

Yasmin Kafai, Psychological Studies in Education, University of California, Los Angeles

Nancy Butler Songer, University of Michigan

D
Workshop Participants and Questions Posted on the Internet

D.1 PARTICIPANTS IN THE JANUARY 1997 WORKSHOP

Robert B. Allen, Bellcore
Robert H. Anderson, RAND
Ronald E. Anderson, University of Minnesota
Robert M. Ballard, North Carolina Central University
Alan W. Biermann, Duke University
Tony Brewer, Pivot Partners
Peter P. Chen, Louisiana State University
Martin Dickey, University of Washington
Linda S. Dobb, Bowling Green State University
Michael B. Eisenberg, Syracuse University and ERIC Clearinghouse on
     Information and Technology
Zorana Ercegovac, University of California, Los Angeles
Susan Gerhart, Applied Formal Methods, Inc. and ROI Joint Venture
Stephen A.B. Gilbert, Massachusetts Institute of Technology
Connie Hendrix, San Francisco Unified School District
Charles F. Kelemen, Swarthmore College
Allen Klinger, University of California, Los Angeles
Susan Landau, University of Massachusetts
Larry Long, Long and Associates

Note: Pointers to many of the position papers presented by these participants can be found online at <http://www2.nas.edu/cstbweb>.

Ellen Meltzer, University of California, Berkeley
David G. Messerschmitt, University of California, Berkeley
Jeanine Meyer, Pace University
Paul Nielson, Manitoba Library Association
Jim Perry, Kinko's Inc.
Viera K. Proulx, Northeastern University
Richard S. Rosenberg, University of British Columbia
Linda Loos Scarth, Mount Mercy College
Greg W. Scragg, State University of New York at Geneseo
Mary Shaw, Carnegie Mellon University
Ralph D. Westfall, University of Southern California
Marsha Cook Woodbury, University of Illinois, Urbana-Champaign

D.2   QUESTIONS ABOUT INFORMATION TECHNOLOGY LITERACY POSTED ON THE INTERNET

D.2.1   Questions for Computer and Communications Scientists and Engineers

1. For purposes of this discussion, the committee provisionally distinguishes in a loose and informal way between fundamental concepts, applications of fundamental concepts, and engineering and design principles used in applying concepts. To illustrate, a concept might be "instruction interpretation." An application of that concept might be "Java byte-code interpretation." An engineering principle might be "design under constraint" (e.g., designing a Java interpreter under the constraint of limited memory or bandwidth).

1a. What are the fundamental concepts of information technology that an educated adult should know? (Interpret information technology broadly to include computing and communications.) For each concept:

- Describe it;
- Identify the age or educational level at which you believe it should first be introduced; and
- Explain how it might be introduced.

1b. What are the essential applications of the fundamental concepts?

- Describe it;
- Identify the age or educational level at which you believe it should first be introduced; and
- Explain how it might be introduced.

1c. What are the essential engineering and/or design principles relevant to information technology?

- Describe it;
- Identify the age or educational level at which you believe it should first be introduced; and
- Explain how it might be introduced.

2.   How do you expect the essential concepts, applications, and engineering/design principles described in your answers to change over time (as information technology evolves)? How should the pedagogical process deal with such changes? How can/should individuals be taught to learn about how to use new and never-before-seen computational artifacts (e.g., new applications, services, hardware devices, software packages)?

3.   How should concepts and skills be balanced in information technology literacy? How do/should concepts and skills complement each other in information technology literacy? How do they compete with each other? In other words, how and to what extent is there a trade-off in learning about concepts versus skills? (For purposes of this discussion, the committee regards a "skill" as facility with a specific computational tool or artifact such as a spreadsheet.)

4.   How can individuals best learn the limitations of information technology? How can they learn to make informed personal/social/policy decisions about issues that involve information technology?

D.2.2 Questions for Employers and Labor Professionals

1.   What information technology skills and knowledge will workers need to do their jobs in the early 21st century? Please indicate whether the perspective from which you are answering this question is that of manufacturing or services, and provide separate answers for entry-level, midlevel, technical-level, and executive-level positions. (For purposes of this discussion, a "skill" is "facility with a specific computational tool or artifact such as a spreadsheet." "Knowledge" might be something like "knowledge of programming," though not necessarily knowledge of a specific programming language.) An example of an entry-level skill might be "data input and use of the Internet." Skills required in mid-level positions might include word processing, database, and spreadsheet skills. An executive-level skill might be the use of teleconferencing. (These examples are intended only as possible illustrations.)

2.   The generic competencies underlying the workplace of the 21st century are generally thought to include project planning, budgeting and scheduling, using/communicating/organizing information, understanding/monitoring systems, and interpersonal skills. In your view, how should workers use computers and telecommunications technology in these five domains? (For example, today a person involved in planning might use spreadsheets, project planners, and flow charts. A person using and organizing information might use word processor or presentation software. A person exercising interpersonal skills might use decision support software.)

3.   What is the mix of general and specific knowledge of information technology that you expect to seek in new entry-level hires? More specifically:

  • What artifacts do you need them to know about?
  • What ability to use new information technology do you expect or need them to have?
  • Should these individuals acquire such knowledge and skills from in-house employer training, informal education, or in some other venue? Why?

4.   What learning or educational experiences would best prepare the employees most likely to be hired? What would enable them to cope with future technological changes and information technology tools with which they have no previous experience?

D.2.3   Literacy Project: Questions for K-12 and Post-Secondary Educators

1.   What should information technology (IT)-literate individuals be prepared to do in the future?   What sorts of lifelong personal, career, and policy decisions should such individuals be prepared to make?   Why? (By "IT literacy," we mean not only an IT-literate person's ability to effectively use computers and other information technology tools, but also his or her understanding of how such technology works, and the role of such technology in society.)

2.   What should all high school graduates/students know about information technology to achieve information technology literacy? Please describe each element of this knowledge (e.g., how to troubleshoot a soft-

ware problem or how to make an informed decision about a public policy decision that involves information technology) and briefly say why you believe this is important. For each element, suggest what about it you believe should be taught at what grade levels.

3.   What learning experiences do students need to achieve the technological literacy described in answer to question 2? ("Learning experiences" can include both in-school and out-of-school activities.) Please be specific, using examples from your own teaching if possible.

4.   What technological environment (computers, networks, software, resources, etc.) do pre-college teachers need to teach technological literacy? What is the minimum technological environment needed today? What is the ideal technological environment needed today? Why? Please describe the relationship of the elements you provided in Question 2 to the nature of this environment. (For example, what kinds of computers or connections to the Internet are minimally adequate?)

D.2.4   Questions for Librarians

1.   In an online information community, what should every citizen know about information technology in order to make effective use of the capabilities it enables? Please describe each element of this knowledge (e.g., how to perform an Internet search, how to understand its results) and briefly say why you believe this is important. For each element, suggest what about it you believe should be taught at what grade levels.

2.   Two particularly important examples of new capabilities are those of information searching and information presentation. What are the basic principles that guide an effective search or presentation? At what level should these principles be taught? How should people learn about the limitations of searches and presentations?

3.   What learning experiences do students need to obtain the skills and knowledge described in answer to Questions 1 and 2? (Learning experiences can include both in-school and out-of-school activities.) Please be specific, using examples from your own teaching if possible.

4.   What technological environment (computers, networks, software, resources, etc.) is needed to support the learning experiences described in Question 3?

D.2.5   Questions for Commercial and Business Information Technologists (e.g., MIS Support, Chief Information Officers)

1.   What will every worker need to know about information technology in order to make effective use of the capabilities it enables? It might be useful to distinguish between information technology skills (i.e., "facility with a specific computational tool or artifact such as a spreadsheet") and knowledge (i.e., "knowledge of programming," though not necessarily knowledge of a specific programming language). Please describe each element of this required knowledge and these required skills.

2.   The generic competencies underlying the workplace of the 21st century are generally thought to include project planning, budgeting and scheduling, using/communicating/organizing information, understanding/monitoring systems, and interpersonal skills. In your view, how should workers use computers and telecommunications technology in these five domains? (For example, today a person involved in planning might use spreadsheets, project planners, and flow charts. A person using and organizing information might use word processor or presentation software. A person exercising interpersonal skills might use decision support software.)

3.   What is the mix of general and specific knowledge of information technology that you expect to see in new employees? More specifically:

   • What specific artifacts (e.g., spreadsheets, word processors) do you need them to know about?
   • What ability to use new information technology do you expect or need them to have?
   • What conceptual knowledge is essential?

   How does your answer change with the employee's seniority in the organization? Should these individuals acquire such knowledge and skills from in-house employer training, in formal or informal education, or in some other venue? Why?

4.   What learning or educational experiences would enable the employees you support to cope with future technological changes and information technology tools with which they have no previous experience?

APPENDIX

E

Members of the Committee

Lawrence Snyder, *Chair,* has been a professor of computer science and engineering at the University of Washington since 1983, following faculty appointments at Purdue University and Yale University. He has been a visiting scholar, Massachusetts Institute of Technology and Harvard University (1987-1988), and a visiting professor at Sydney University, Sydney, Australia (1994-1995). Dr. Snyder received his Ph.D. from Carnegie Mellon University in computer science (1973) and a B.A. from the University of Iowa in mathematics and economics (1968). Dr. Snyder has served on the Computer Research Association's board of directors and on numerous advisory panels formulating future research directions in VLSI technology and parallel computation. He is co-founder and general chair of the ACM's Symposium on Parallel Algorithms and Architectures. He chaired the CSTB's study on academic careers of experimental computer science and engineering; he also serves on the NRC's Army Research Laboratory Technical Assessment Board. Dr. Snyder is a fellow of the IEEE and a fellow of the ACM.

Alfred V. Aho is associate research vice president, Communications Sciences Research, at Bell Laboratories, Lucent Technologies. From 1995 to 1997, he was a professor in and chair of the Computer Science Department at Columbia University, and from 1991 to 1995 he was the general manager of the Information Sciences and Technologies Research Laboratory at Bellcore. Prior to holding these appointments, he was director of the Computing Science Research Center at Bell Laboratories from 1987 to 1991. He joined Bell Laboratories in 1967 as a member of the technical staff in the Computing Techniques Research Department, and in 1980 he was appointed head of the Computing Principles Research Department. Dr. Aho received a B.A.Sc. (engineering physics, 1963) from the University of Toronto and a Ph.D. (electrical engineering/computer science, 1967) from Princeton University. Dr. Aho's personal research is centered on data networking, multimedia information systems, database systems and query languages, programming languages and their compilers, algorithms, and the theory of computing. He has published more than 60 technical papers and ten widely used textbooks in these areas. He is a co-inventor of the AWK programming language and other UNIX system tools. Dr. Aho is a fellow of the ACM, the American Association for the Advancement of Science, Bell Laboratories, and the IEEE. He is a former chair of the ACM's SIGACT and a former member of the Computer Science and Telecommunications Board.

Marcia C. Linn is professor of development and cognition and of education in mathematics, science, and technology in the Graduate School of Education at the University of California, Berkeley. A fellow of the American Association for the Advancement of Science, she researches the teaching and learning of science and technology, gender equity, and the design of technological learning environments. In 1998, the Council of Scientific Society Presidents selected her for its first award in educational research. From 1995-1996 she was a fellow at the Center for Advanced Study in the Behavioral Sciences. In 1994, the National Association for Research in Science Teaching presented her with its Award for Lifelong Distinguished Contributions to Science Education. The American Educational Research Association bestowed on her the Willystine Goodsell Award in 1991 and the Women Educator's Research Award in 1982. Twice she has won the Outstanding Paper Award of the *Journal of Research in Science Teaching* (1975 and 1983). She has served on the board of the American Association for the Advancement of Science, the Graduate Record Examination Board of the Educational Testing Service, and the McDonnell Foundation Cognitive Studies in Education Practice board. Her publications include *Computers, Teachers, Peers – Science Learning Partners*, with Sherry Hsi (Lawrence Erlbaum & Associates, in press); "Key to the Information Highway" in *Communications of the Association for Computing Machinery* (1996); "The Tyranny of the Mean: Gender and Expectations" in *Notices of the American Mathematical Society* (1994); *Designing Pascal Solutions*, with M.C. Clancy (W.H. Freeman, 1992); and "The Case for Case Studies in Programming Instruction," with M.C. Clancy in *Communications of the Association for Computing Machinery* (1992).

Arnold H. Packer is a senior fellow at the Institute for Policy Studies at Johns Hopkins University and recently served as executive director of the U.S. Labor Department Secretary's Commission on Achieving Necessary Skills (SCANS). He is currently chair of the SCANS/2000 Center. Dr. Packer has extensive experience in the fields of restructuring U.S. education and policymaking and is co-author of *Workforce 2000*, a publication that has influenced the national conversation about human resource education. He has worked extensively with distinguished representatives from business, labor, education, and government to define the skills needed by all high school graduates to succeed in the workplace. Dr. Packer previously served as the assistant secretary for Policy, Evaluation, and Research at the U.S. Department of Labor, where he formulated the administration's approach to work-based welfare reform and to retraining workers dislocated by economic change. His most recent book is *School-to-Work: Reinventing the Learning Enterprise.*

Allen B. Tucker is professor of computer science at Bowdoin College; he has held similar positions at Colgate University and Georgetown University. He served for 16 years as department chair in these institutions and 2 years as associate dean of the faculty. He held the John D. and Catherine T. MacArthur Chair in Computer Science while at Colgate from 1983 to 1988. Professor Tucker earned a B.A. in mathematics from Wesleyan University in 1963 and an M.S. and Ph.D. in computer science from Northwestern University in 1970. He is the author or co-author of several books and articles in the areas of programming languages, natural language processing, and computer science education. He has also served as a consultant to several colleges, universities, and other public and private institutions, in several areas of computer science curriculum, software design, programming languages, and natural language processing application. A fellow of the ACM, Professor Tucker co-chaired the ACM/IEEE-CS Joint Curriculum Task Force that developed "Curricula 1991," for which he received the ACM's Outstanding Contribution Award and shared the IEEE's Meritorious Service Award. Most recently, he served as Editor-in-Chief of the 2600-page *CRC Handbook of Computer Science and Engineering* (CRC Press, 1997), a comprehensive professional handbook that covers the entire discipline. He is a member of the ACM, the IEEE Computer Society, Computer Professionals for Social Responsibility, and the Liberal Arts Computer Science (LACS) Consortium.

Jeffrey Ullman has been a professor at Stanford University since 1979. He has also served as a visiting professor at the University of California, Berkeley, and as an Einstein Fellow at the Hebrew University in Jerusalem. Dr. Ullman is a member of several professional organizations and has functioned as the chair at numerous symposiums including the ACM Symposium on Principles of Programming Languages and the Technion International Symposium on Machines and Computations. Dr. Ullman has served on the National Science Foundation Panel on Computer Science and was the chair of the Examination Committee for the CS GRE. Dr. Ullman is the author and co-author of more than ten books and of several journal articles. He received his B.S. in engineering mathematics from Columbia University in 1963 and his Ph.D. in electrical engineering from Princeton University in 1966.

Andries van Dam is Thomas J. Watson, Jr., University Professor of Technology and Education and professor of computer science at Brown University, and was one of the Computer Science Department's founders and its first chair, from 1979 to 1985. His research has concerned computer graphics, text processing, and hypermedia systems. He has been working for more than 30 years on systems for creating and reading electronic books for use in teaching and research. The current project in this research, Exploratories, addresses the educational challenges implicit in a rapidly changing, Web-based environment. An exploratory is a computer-based combination of an exploratorium and a laboratory that embeds in a hypermedia environment a multifaceted interactive microworld that models objects, phenomena, and concepts. In addition, he has been concerned with teaching object-oriented programming and design, including elementary design patterns, in an introductory computer science course. Professor van Dam received the B.S. degree with honors from Swarthmore College in 1960 and the M.S. and Ph.D. from the University of Pennsylvania in 1963 and 1966, respectively. He co-founded ACM SIGGRAPH, has been on the editorial board and served as editor of several computer graphics journals, and is on the technical advisory board of several startups and of Microsoft Research. His honors include these: 1974, the Society for Information Display's Special Recognition Award; 1984, the IEEE Centennial Medal; 1988, the State of Rhode Island Governor's Science and Technology Award; 1990, the National Computer Graphics Association's Academic Award; 1991, SIGGRAPH's Steven A. Coons Award; 1994, the Karl V. Karlstrom Outstanding Educator Award, the IEEE Fellow Award, and the ACM Fellow Award; 1996, elected to the National Academy of Engineering; 1999, IEEE James H. Mulligan, Jr. Education Medal.